Lynn D. £5-60

MASSACHUSETTS
A PICTURE MEMORY

Text
Bill Harris

Captions
Pauline Graham

Design
Teddy Hartshorn

Photography
Amstock
Colour Library Books Ltd
Karen Kent

Picture Editor
Annette Lerner

Commissioning Editor
Andrew Preston

Editorial
Gill Waugh
David Gibbon

Production
Ruth Arthur
Sally Connolly
David Proffit
Andrew Whitelaw

Director of Production
Gerald Hughes

CLB 2676
© 1991 Colour Library Books Ltd, Godalming, Surrey, England.
All rights reserved.
This 1991 edition published by Crescent Books,
distributed by Outlet Book Company, Inc, a Random House Company,
225 Park Avenue South, New York, New York 10003.
Color separations by Tien Wah Press Pte Ltd, Singapore.
Printed and bound in Singapore.
ISBN 0 517 06025 6
8 7 6 5 4 3 2 1

MASSACHUSETTS
A PICTURE MEMORY

CRESCENT BOOKS
NEW YORK

First page: Marconi Beach, Wellfleet, Cape Cod. From here, on January 18, 1903, Guglielmo Marconi sent the first radio signal across the Atlantic. Previous pages: Provincetown, Cape Cod, where the Pilgrims first landed on November 21, 1620. Facing page: Daniel Chester French's statue Minute Man, *standing at the western end of the North Bridge, Concord.*

Nobody knows how long they stayed or why they left, but the first people to settle in Massachusetts seem to have arrived around 10,000 B.C. They knew how to use tools and developed a very effective spear for hunting. There were plenty of animals to provide them with food and, though they weren't farmers, there were enough wild fruit- and nut-bearing trees and bushes to vary their diet. But after a thousand years or so they vanished. They might have been victims of an epidemic or a war or just plain wanderlust. But they left the place almost unchanged, with hardly a clue that they had ever been there. And if there were storytellers among them who told tales of their ancestral home, there were apparently no outsiders listening. The next human settlers didn't arrive until more than 5,000 years later.

They were the forerunners of the great Algonquin Nation that eventually extended north to Labrador, south to Cape Hatteras and west into present-day Michigan and Illinois. Though they shared a basic language and a common ancestry, like many families they didn't always see eye-to-eye with one another, and they were as good at making war as they were at hunting and scratching out a living from a land that still seems determined to resist the plow.

The Algonquins were hunters first and foremost and generally considered farming so onerous that it was only fit for women to do. There is no evidence that any of the women ever complained, but not because they didn't have reason to. They had no way of knowing it, but nature began conspiring against them half a million years earlier. During four separate epochs the northern part of the continent was covered with thick glaciers that scraped unmercifully at the land. The last of them, known as the Wisconsin Glacier, created the Massachusetts we know today.

As it inched forward from the northwest it finished the job of grinding down

Alpine-sized mountains and sweeping away the sediment as many as fifteen feet below the surface. The ice was heavy enough to grind boulders into sand and to move huge rocks hundreds of miles. Super-hard rocks that resisted the onslaught still stand today as monadnocks, the isolated mountains that add interest to the otherwise flat landscape the ice sheet created. And in some places where the rocks offered more resistance, the ice moved around them and dug out deep valleys. When the climate changed and the ice began to melt much of the debris under it was deposited in the form of moraines, and the water that rushed down its sides spread the rest of it along the plains. The meltwater created the rivers that are still flowing, but it also raised the level of the sea, which swallowed up mile after mile of the land and in the process created the offshore shoals that would plague mariners for generations.

The weight of the ice sheets had forced the overall level of the land to sink more than 1,500 feet, and when the millions of tons of ice was removed the surface rose again high enough to hold back the sea. But in some places the glacier had done its work too well and the Atlantic moved inland to create Nantucket Sound, Buzzards Bay and Massachusetts Bay. Cape Cod and the offshore islands, left behind as the tops of higher than average moraines, escaped drowning, but the sea has been at work changing their shape ever since.

Once the familiar outlines were established the work began in earnest. Vegetation appeared on the coastal plain and left its remains behind to enrich the sand. But even after centuries, except in low places where ponds and bogs had formed, it was still as barren as a desert. Any rain that fell was swallowed up by the loose soil and absorbed by the granite a few feet under the surface. A few miles inland the landscape gave way to low hills studded with ponds, and then eventually to mountains a thousand or more feet high. They had escaped the full impact of the glaciers, but not to the extent that the hillsides weren't littered with rocks and boulders. The ice also left a legacy in the form of deep river valleys that carried off the thin soil from the slopes above them. It all added up to a countryside that, though beautiful, never was the end of the rainbow for anyone interested in farming.

By the time the Indians began arriving, the territory we call Massachusetts looked very much like it does today. But, like the white men who would follow them, they did what they could to change it. In the winter months they migrated into the inland valleys, where game was more plentiful and easier to find when the leaves were off the trees. But in summer, just as New Englanders do today, they moved closer to the shore, where the women busied themselves clearing fields and planting crops while the men went about their business of hunting and fishing. And just to make the odds a little better, they routinely burned away the underbrush that might give cover to the small animals they hunted. After a season or two, when the fields began producing less corn and grain, they moved to a different spot and created even more open land. By the time the whites began moving into their midst, the forests that might in time have enriched the coastal plain had been cleared. But if the Native Americans had thwarted nature's plan, they made life a whole lot easier for the intruders.

The entire area was eventually named for the Massachusetts, the tribe that made its home along the coast in the area near present-day Boston. But they weren't the only tribe in the region. The Wampanoags lived between Narragansett Bay and the ocean and along Buzzards Bay. Cape Cod was the home of the Nausets, and north of Cape Ann were the Pennacooks, whose neighbors further north, the Abnakis, were generally at war with them. The center of the present state was the territory of the Nipmunks, and the river valleys to their south were occupied by the Pocumtucks. Out west, the Berkshires belonged to the Mahicans, although the idea that they owned the hills would have puzzled them. They had no concept of land ownership that matched the beliefs of the English, but each tribe stayed within its own territory and each family seems to have had hereditary rights to hunting grounds and the land they cultivated.

They had no way of knowing it, but their world began to unravel in 1602, when thirty-two would-be settlers led by Bartholomew Gosnold sailed around Cape Cod and into Nantucket Sound, eventually deciding to establish a colony on Cuttyhunk, one of the Elizabeth Islands. They lost their enthusiasm in less than three weeks and sailed back home to England. Several other explorers followed them and each in his turn published glowing accounts of the Massachusetts coast. Many noted that the soil was too thin for productive farming and their descriptions of the cold winters sent the next waves of would-be settlers in the direction of Virginia. Among them was a breakaway group of Puritans who called themselves Separatists. They were being hounded out of England for their radical ideas and negotiated with the Virginia Company to relocate in North America. They arrived in early November, 1620, not at Virginia, but much further north at the tip of Cape Cod.

The first Indians they saw were Nausets, but only at a distance. In a few weeks they sailed across Cape Cod Bay and into Wampanoag territory. They were lucky enough to find an abandoned village that had been home to the Patuxets, a tribe that had been wiped out by a plague, quite possibly imported from Europe by the earlier explorers. They were also lucky to find the natives friendly. They had hardly settled down at the spot they called Plymouth when they were visited by two Indians, Squanto and Samoset, both of whom had been taken to England by a party of explorers, and before being returned home again had become fluent in English. Once contact was made, it was only a matter of time before the Pilgrims were visited by the Wampanoag sachem, Massasoit, who signed a treaty of peace and mutual cooperation that lasted another fifty years. It wasn't a one-sided agreement. In return for the Indians' help, the Pilgrims gave them the benefit of their tiny, armed militia against the Narragansetts who lived to the south and had been casting lustful eyes on Massasoit's domain.

Over the next several years, other Separatists arrived to expand the Plymouth colony, but a half-dozen other groups tried to establish themselves on the Massachusetts coast and usually failed. By 1630 the survivors were strung out up the coast and into Maine, quite unaware that they about to be swallowed up by the Puritan juggernaut. Within the next decade, an average of a thousand Englishmen a year would follow the lead of John Winthrop and emigrate to America through Boston harbor.

Winthrop and his followers were quite different from other would-be colonists. They were able to make Boston the headquarters of their company, and they didn't have to go back to London to have important decisions made. And Winthrop and his fellow proprietors were men of wealth. The first flotilla of sixteen ships that in 1630 brought a thousand settlers, along with all the necessities of life, cost the Massachusetts Bay Company more than £200,000, an investment in today's dollars of well over fifty million. But as far as the Puritans were concerned, it was money well spent.

It's easy to sum up their intentions in settling Massachusetts Bay as a search for "religious freedom," but it was actually quite different from that. The Separatists who had already moved to Plymouth were militants who thought the established church was so corrupt that it needed to be fought from the outside. Their neighbors fought back, and they found themselves forced out of the society they wanted to change. The more conservative Puritans wanted change, too, but worked from within the Establishment to make it happen. They weren't exactly beloved for their attempts to purify the church in England, but they had the freedom to get on with their efforts and, in fact, many Puritans were opposed to moving away because they thought their goal was in sight. But men like John Winthrop had a deeper motive. They found their neighbors self-serving and businessmen in general deceitful. They thought that men with power were abusing it, and that England was well on its way to calling the wrath of God down on itself. They decided among themselves that God had finally led explorers to the New World as a means of revealing a place where the faithful could escape the coming holocaust, and that by transplanting themselves to North America they could establish an example that might eventually save England from the wickedness that was surely going to destroy it.

The more Winthrop thought about it, the more convinced he became that God had chosen the Puritans to implement a divine plan, and that settling Massachusetts was nothing less than the first step in saving the Christian church from itself as well as from the agents of Satan. He was just as convinced that the Almighty had presented his chosen people with a challenge, and that every hardship would be a test of their faith. It was their responsibility, he told his people, to build a model community that future generations as well as their contemporaries would want to emulate. He also told them that, if they failed, their God would suffer as much as they themselves and that in all probability the whole world would fall before the forces of evil.

There is no dispute that Massachusetts Bay was the most successful colony ever established by English-speaking people. And there is no question that what Americans still consider their most important values first arrived on these shores aboard the ships of the fleet that sailed into Boston Harbor in 1630. The Puritan code followed the pioneers all the way to the Pacific Coast, and it formed the core of the country's basic belief about itself through all of its formative years. In fact, it wasn't until the 1960s that anyone even considered challenging the ideas of the Puritans, even though they themselves had long since faded into the mists of history. But for all their sneering references to the so-called "Protestant Ethic," the new radicals weren't able make it a thing of the past.

But no set of ideas, even if inspired by God himself apparently, is ever perfect. If the Puritans gave America a standard of character, they also gave it a character flaw in their treatment of the Native Americans. They set the pattern for dealing with the Indians in every part of the country through every stage of settlement, and made it possible for whites to break most of the Ten Commandments and believe that it was what God wanted them to do.

The Bible is filled with references to the wilderness as the domain of Satan, and the Puritans took it all to heart. Even if the dark forests beyond their coastal settlement weren't inhabited by wild animals and a savage race of men they represented an evil in themselves. The presence of savages confirmed it. The Indians had never heard of the white man's God, to be sure, but that meant they must be servants of the devil. A man had to be one or the other, after all. Some of the red men were redeemed through conversion to Christianity, but most resisted the opportunity, and even those who agreed that there might be something to be said for this concept of an all-powerful God had a problem with the Puritan idea of godliness. Such things didn't go unnoticed in Boston, and before long the struggle between the civilized Europeans and the Native Americans took on the same aspects as Christ's own struggle against the devil in the wilderness.

In spite of it, hostility was a long time coming and the first blow was struck by the red men themselves. Ironically, they themselves were recent arrivals, Mohicans from the Dutch-controlled Hudson Valley who had forced their way eastward and in the process became known to the local Indians as *Pequot*, "destroyers." When they murdered a white trapper in 1636, armed men went out from Boston to avenge him by attacking a Pequot village. That, in turn, led to a reign of terror that ended when another avenging force from Boston killed five hundred Pequot men, women and children and burned their village to the ground. It sent a strong message to the other tribes in the area, and about a third of them decided to convert to Christianity. A combination of feuding among themselves, which was traditional, and paying lip service to the white man's ways, which was practical, kept the Indians from becoming a problem again for nearly forty more years.

But during those years, the white colonies kept growing and taking away more of the Indian land. The Wampanoags lost the most and by the time old Massasoit died and his son, Philip, became sachem, the young braves had become restless. Philip knew that his father had relied on the Englishmen to protect his people from the Narragansetts, but changed the balance by uniting all the tribes in the area, including the hated Narragansetts. The war that followed lasted slightly longer than a year, with heavy casualties on both sides. When it was over the Narragansett, Wampanoag and Nipmunk tribes had ceased to exist. Many of the surviving warriors and their sachems were tried and executed as war criminals and their women and children taken as household servants in the white settlements. Hundreds of other Indians were sold as slaves in the West Indies.

But if their God was pleased, He didn't shower the Puritans with gratitude. They had enjoyed a kind of "most favored colony" status under Oliver Cromwell's Commonwealth in England. But when the monarchy was restored and the Puritans fell out of favor in London, the new king, Charles II, revoked the Bay Company's charter and began treating Massachusetts like all his other colonies. The colonists didn't exactly take it lying down, and when William and Mary were proclaimed king and queen of England in 1689, they imprisoned the royal governor and seized a British ship in Boston harbor. It was all over quickly, but they made a point. Eighty-six years later they tried again, and became the lynch pin in the establishment of the American nation, a role that would have made the colony's founders justifiably proud. Just exactly one hundred and fifty years after they established their colony at Boston, it became part of the Commonwealth of Massachusetts, U.S.A., and without them those initials might never have come into existence.

In the years since, Massachusetts has never stopped putting its special stamp on the history and the character of America. Towns as far away as the California Coast imitate its architecture. The governments of every locality as well as the Federal Government itself follow its model. Schools in every state follow the pattern established by the earliest Puritans, who felt that no human could be truly saved from the forces of evil without being able to read the word of God. American poetry and literature traces its roots to the sons and daughters of Massachusetts. And the industrial revolution that transformed the country came to America along the streams and beside the waterfalls of Massachusetts. But if it is a culture that is often imitated, the original is alive and well, from the Atlantic Coast to the Berkshire Hills. They are fond of saying that the spirit of Massachusetts is the spirit of America and few boasts are closer to the truth.

"New Church" – the Church of the New Jerusalem – was built and dedicated in 1870 in Yarmouth, Cape Cod. It is also known as the Swedenborgian Church because its members belong to a small sect which follows the scriptural interpretations of Emanuel Swedenborg, a Swedish scientist and mystic of the eithteenth century.

10

Facing page top and above: First Congregational Church in Williams College (right), Williamstown. Below: the Meeting House of Williamstown's First Congregational Church. The site was first settled by soldiers from Fort Massachusetts in 1753. It was later named for Colonel Ephraim Williams Jr., whose bequest enabled the founding of Williams College, chartered in 1793. Facing page bottom: a Deerfield home. Above right: Memorial Hall, Deerfield. Below right: Deerfield Inn.

Below and overleaf: 1725 Dwight Barnard House Museum, Deerfield (these pages). This house originally stood in Springfield, Connecticut. It was moved to Deerfield in 1954. Facing page: (top) Sheldon-Hawks House, circa 1743, and (bottom) the 1730 Reverend Jonathan Ashley House. Ashley was a devoted Tory who persisted in his loyalty to the Crown despite his parishioners trying to bar him from the church.

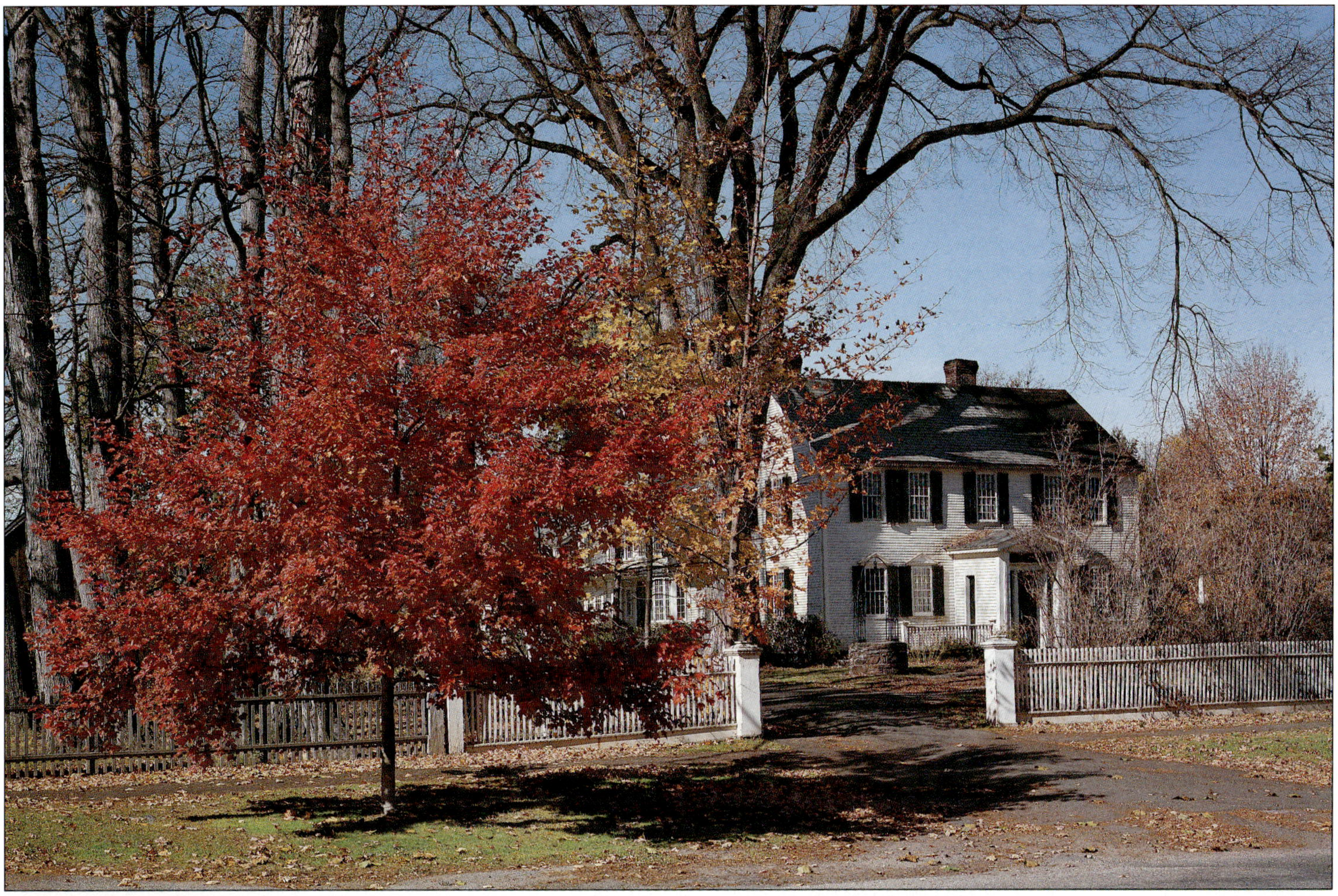

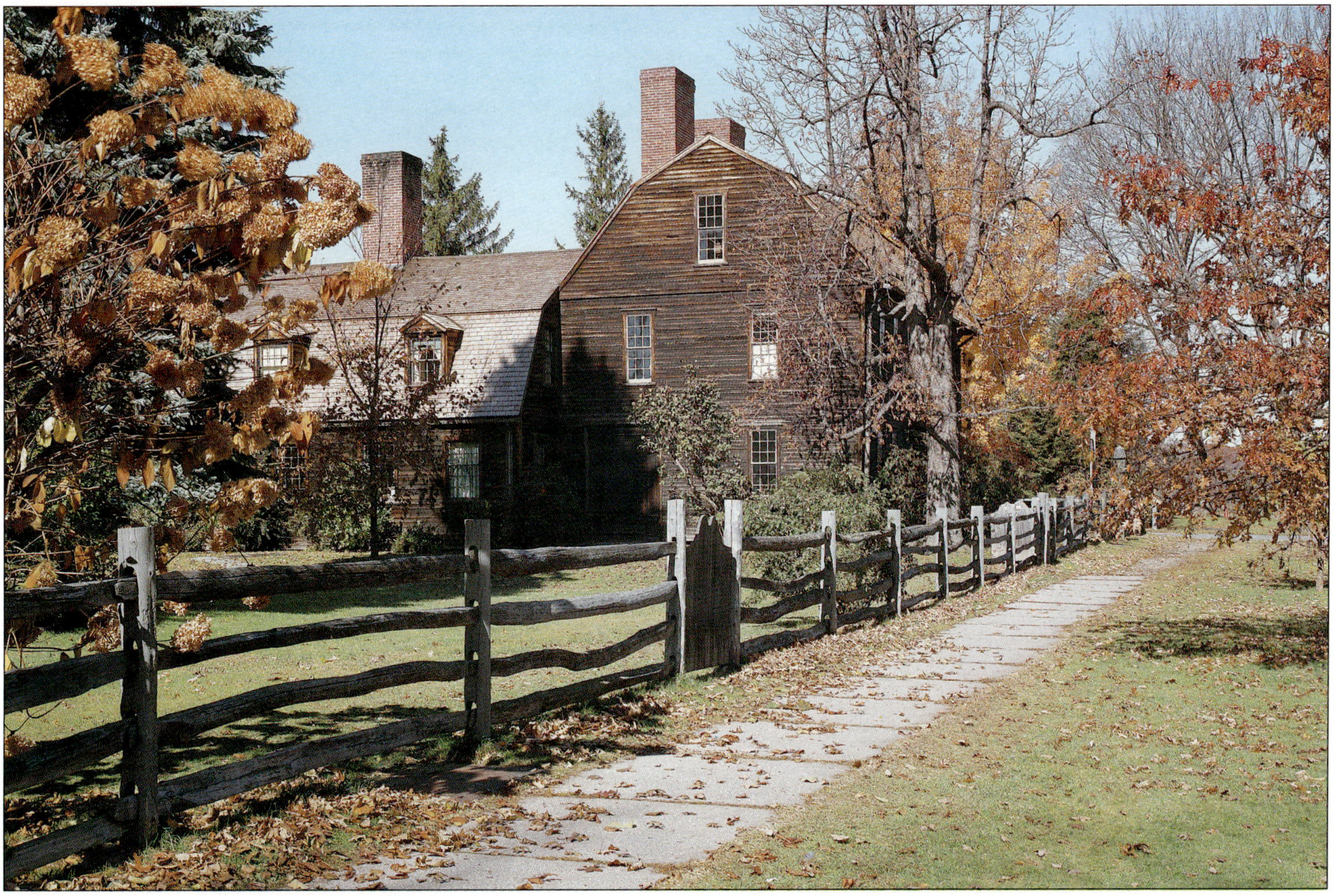

Left: the Sister Shop at Hancock Shaker Village (these pages). The frame outside was used for dipping candles. Below left: the 1830 Brick Dwelling House. It was built with two entrances, one for the women, the other for the men. Bottom left: the barn complex, and (below) the combination Machine Shop and Laundry. Overleaf: the 1826 Shaker Round Barn in Fruitlands Museum, Harvard, in the Berkshires.

Below: a lake near Otis. Facing page: (top) a marina near Williamstown, and (bottom) Upper Sheffield Bridge, the oldest covered bridge in Massachusetts. Sheffield itself, established in 1733, is the oldest town in Berkshire County.

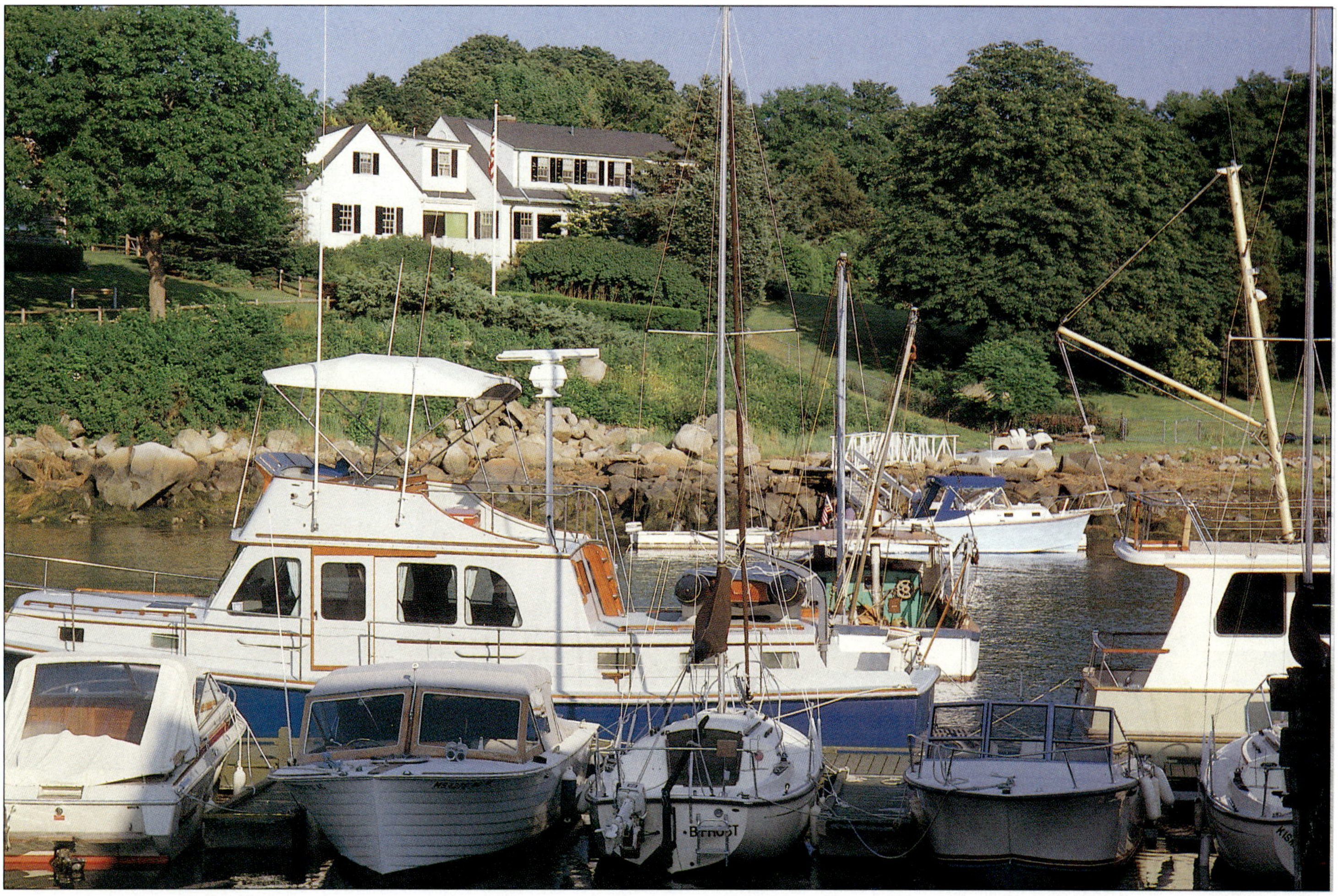

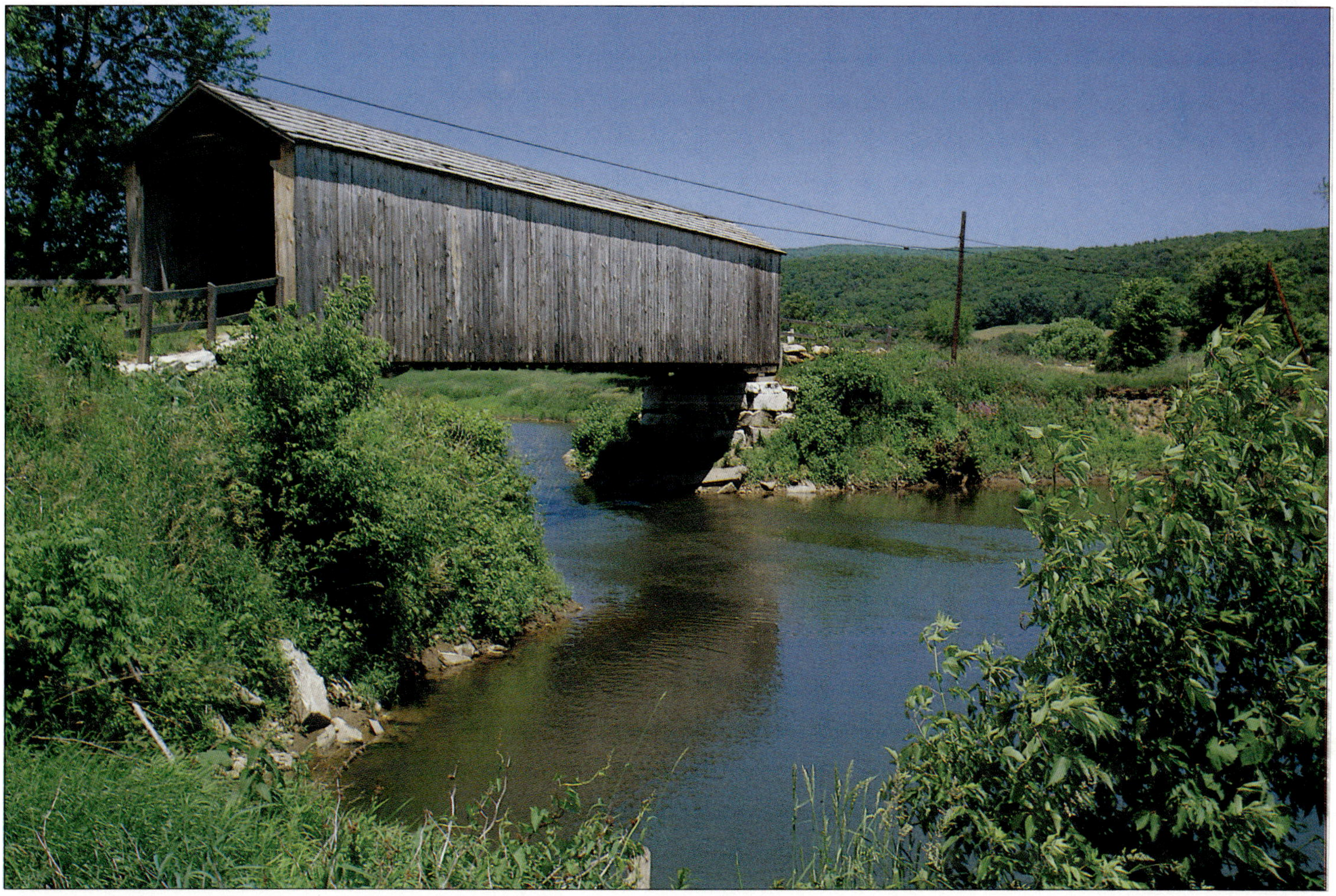

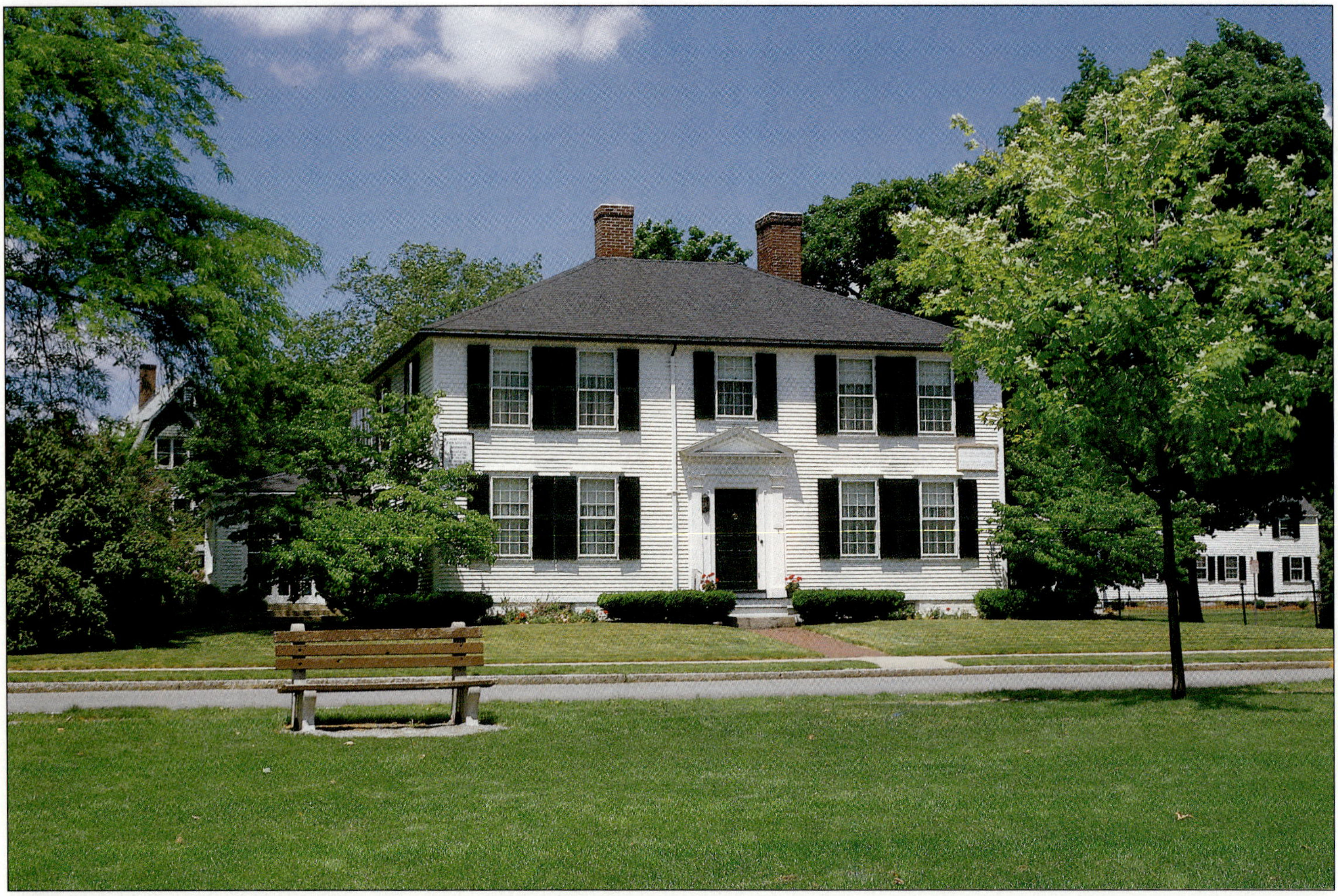

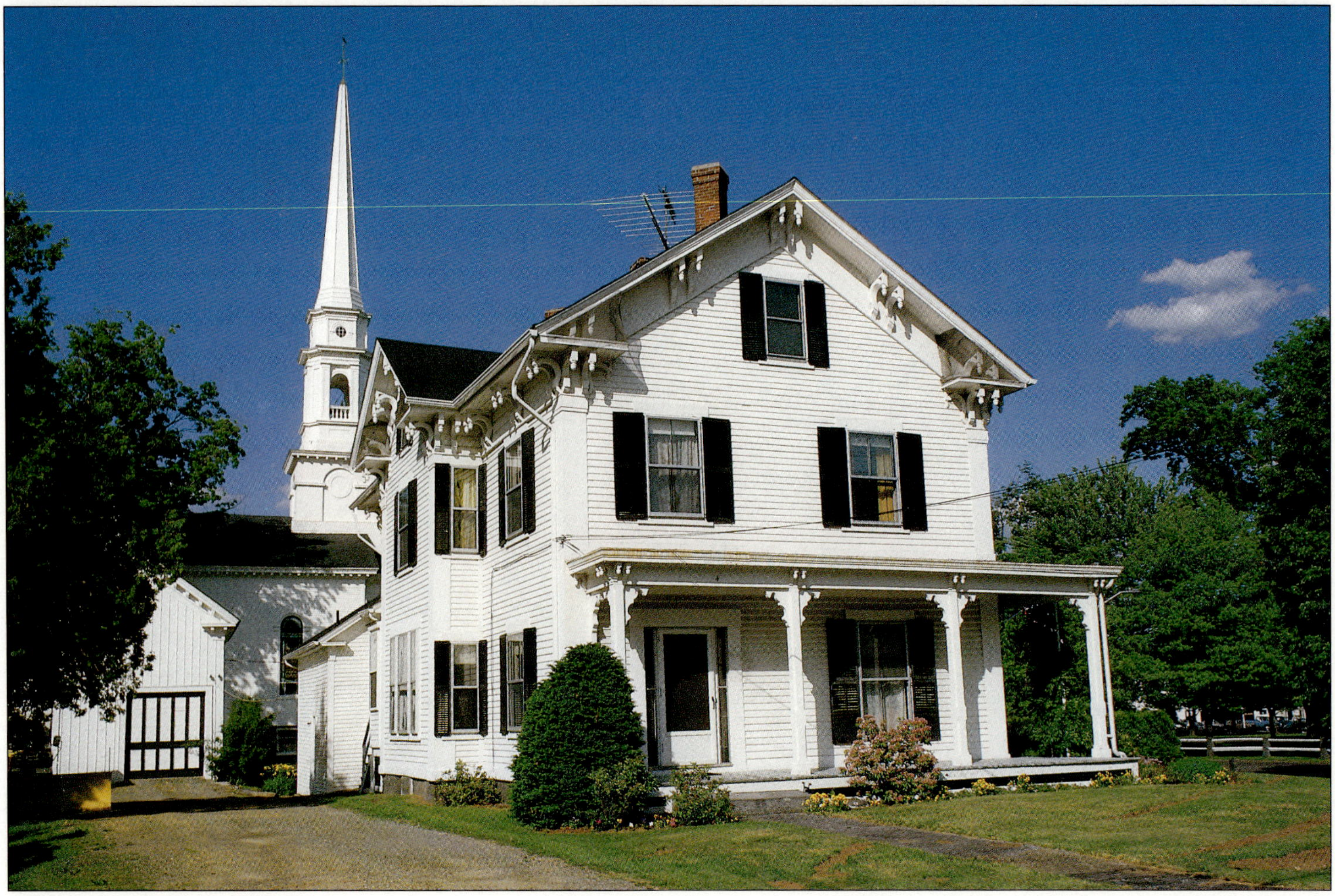

Facing page top and above right: Battle Green, Lexington. This is where Captain John Parker and his Minute Men formed to meet the British troops heralded by Paul Revere. Facing page bottom: a clapboard house in Barre. Above: First Congregational Church, Worthington. Right: Jones Library, Amherst, housing many of the works and manuscripts of Emily Dickinson alongside items belonging to Robert Frost. Below right: the Catholic Church at Amherst. Below: Monterey.

23

Left: Salem Towne House, built in 1796 for the prosperous businessman Salem Towne Sr., in Old Sturbridge Village (these pages). The village opened as a historical center in 1946, the idea of Albert and J. Cheney Wells. Forty historical buildings have been moved to the site since then. Below left: the Pottery. Below: the Richardson Parsonage, a red and white "saltbox" built in 1740 as the home of the village parson.

Below: boardwalk through the Parker River National Wildlife Refuge. Facing page: (top) Rocky Neck, and (bottom) Little Neck. Overleaf: the harbor at Newburyport, an old shipbuilding town on the banks of the Merrimack River.

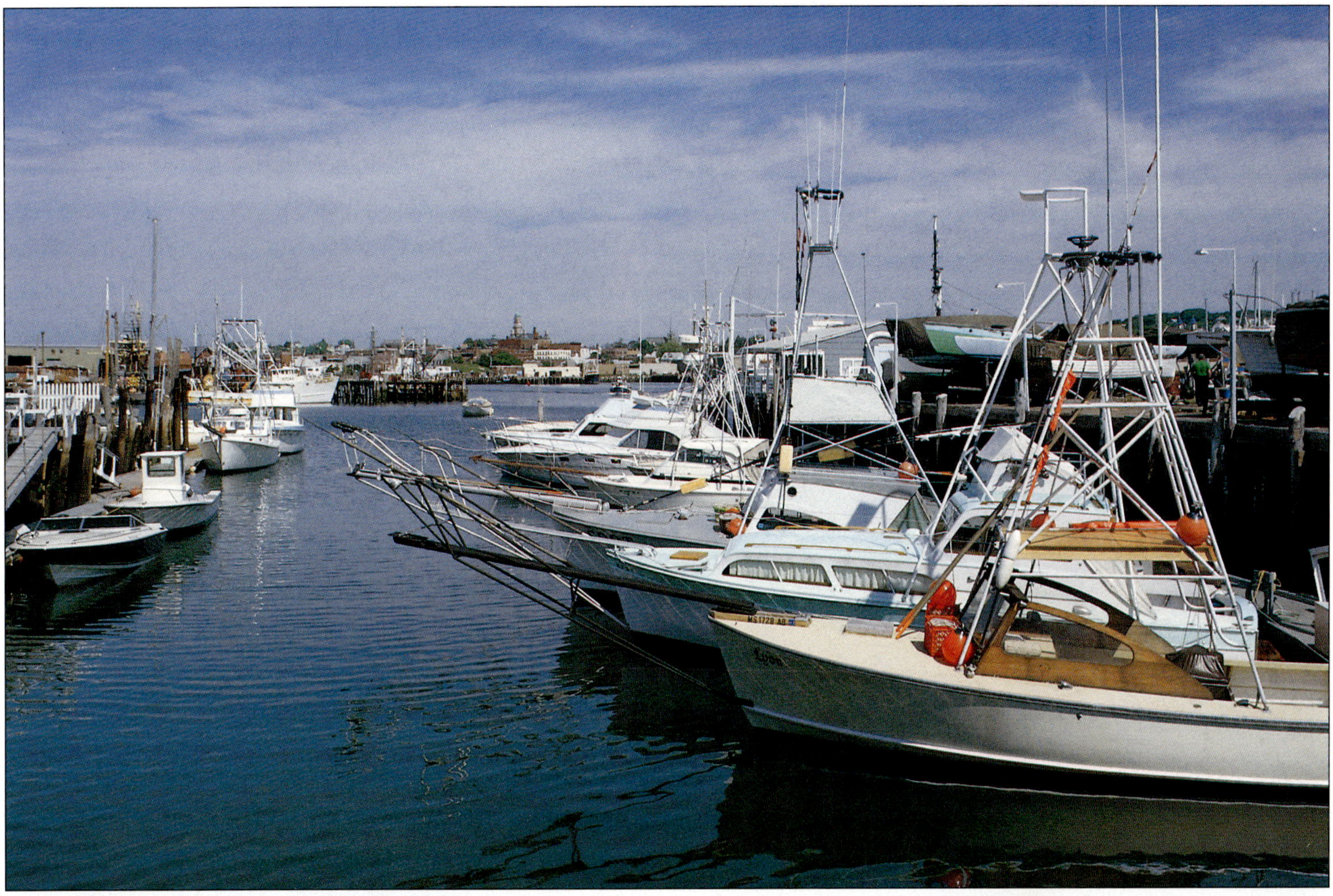

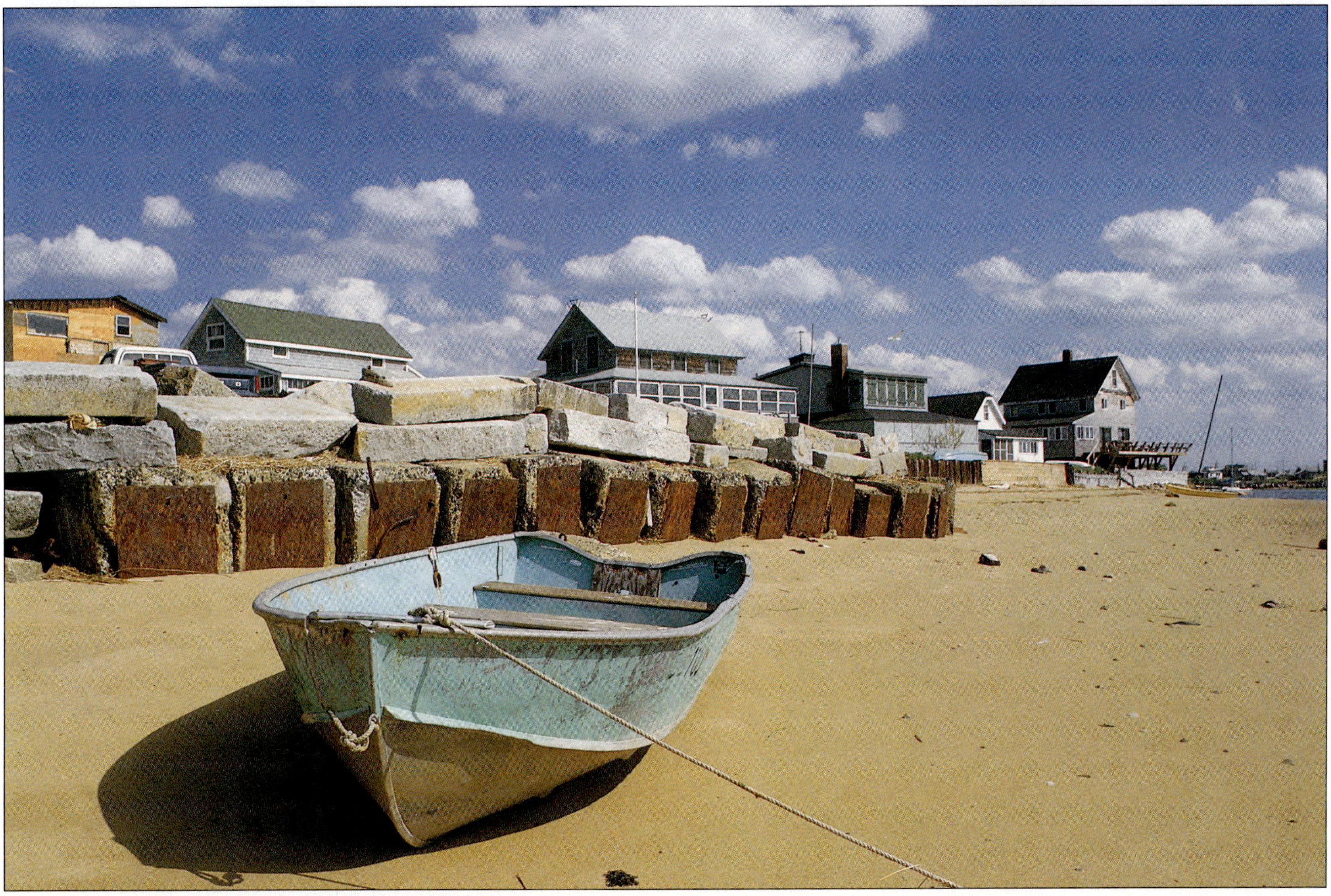

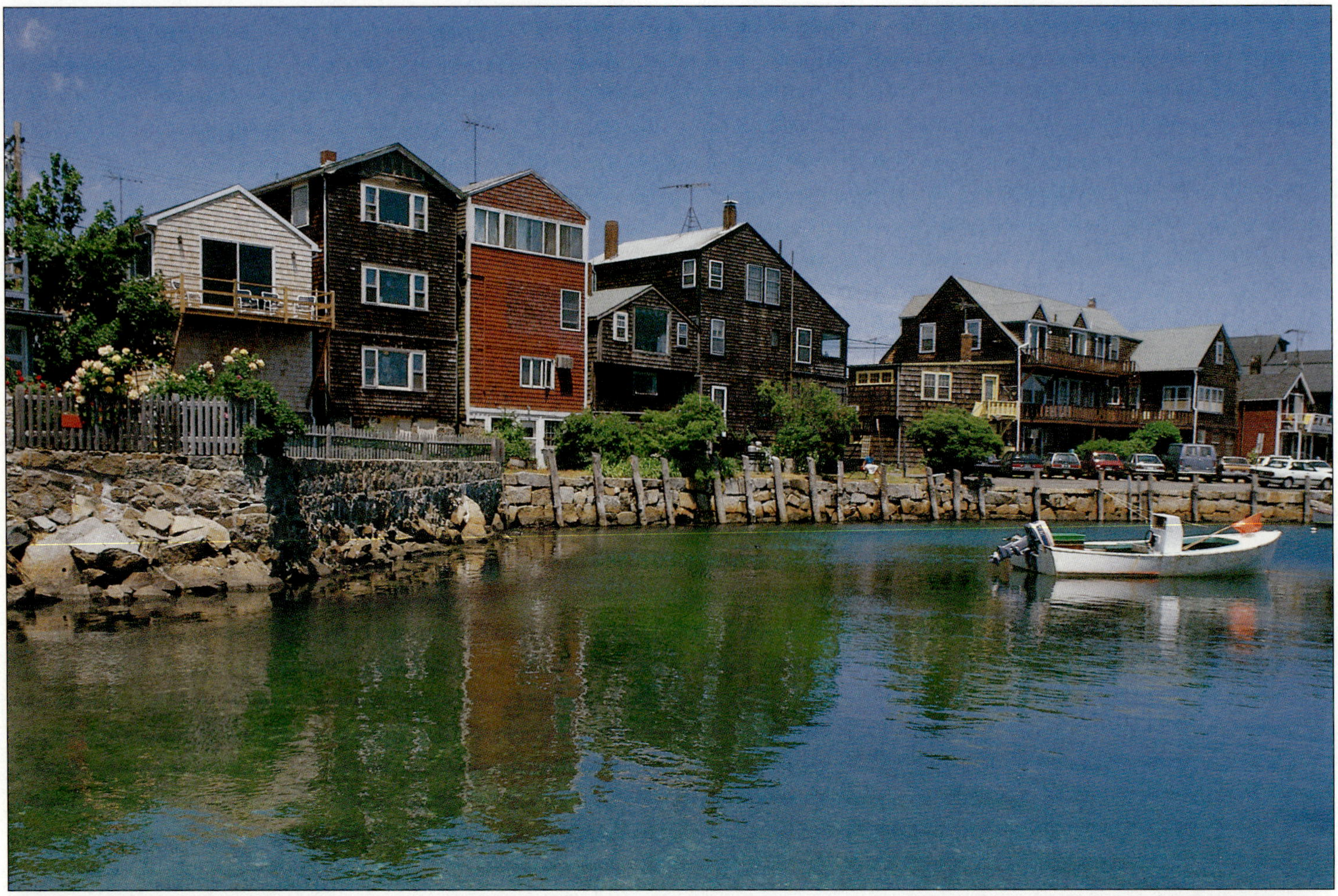

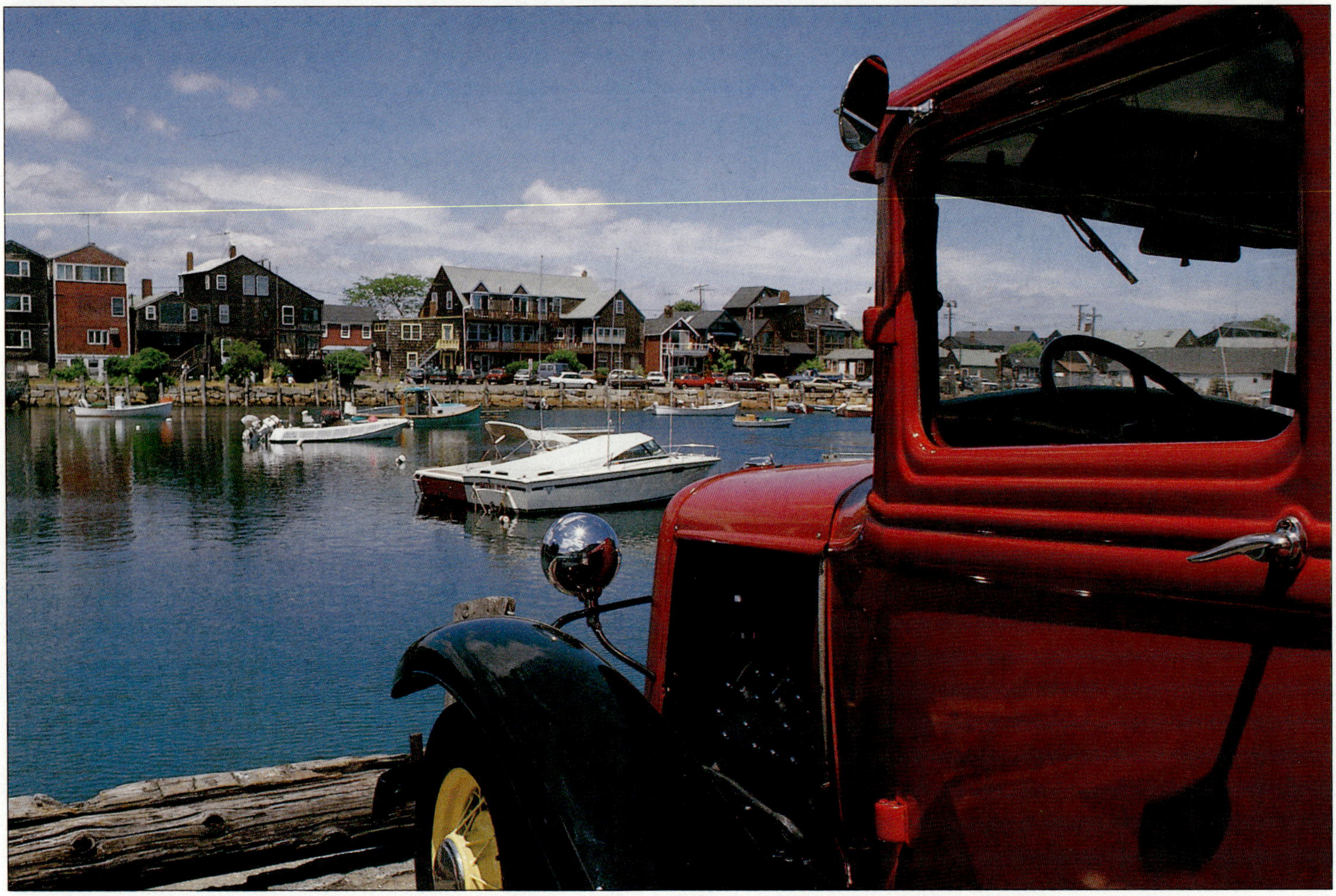

Facing page: Rockport Harbor, and (above) Mosher Gallery, Rockport (these pages). Rockport began as a fishing village, but during the 1920s it developed into an artists' colony. Today this popular resort seems a far cry from the times when granite was quarried from Rockport shores and shipped as far afield as South America. These days visitors swim in the old Lainesville Quarries, now a freshwater pool, from which the stone for many of Boston's buildings once came.

Left: the yachting center of Marblehead, and (below left) a wharf on the Annisquam River. Bottom left: Lanes Cove. Below: the harbor at Gloucester, a thriving fishing port – the oldest seaport in the country. Its fleet of fishing schooners was made famous by Rudyard Kipling in his novel Captains Courageous. *Overleaf: Pickering Wharf, Salem. During the Revolutionary War, Salem sailors captured about 400 British vessels.*

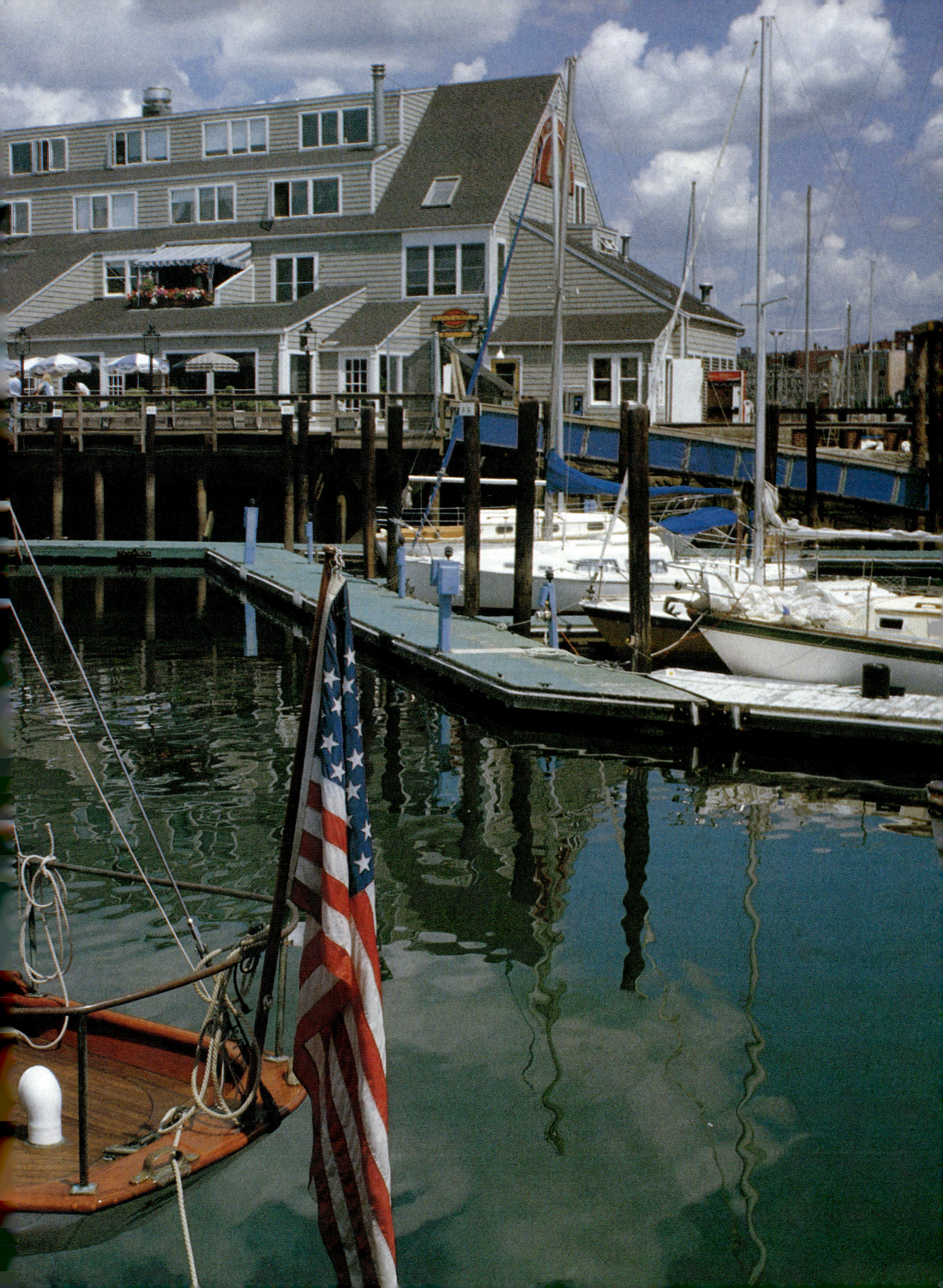

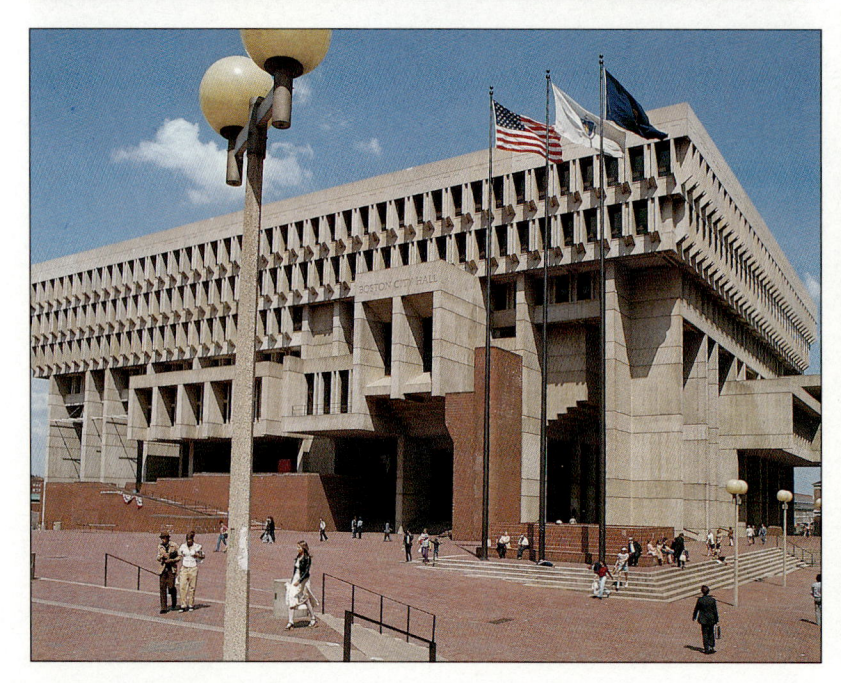

Above and overleaf: the Hancock Tower, Boston (these pages). Above left: Boston Public Garden with Thomas Ball's bronze of George Washington. Left: Massachusetts State House, and (below left) City Hall. The roof of the State House was originally copper leaf, courtesy of Paul Revere. It was re-covered in gold in 1874. Below: Quincy Market. Facing page: (top) Harvard University and its blue-domed Eliot House on the banks of the Charles River, and (bottom) Boston Common.

37

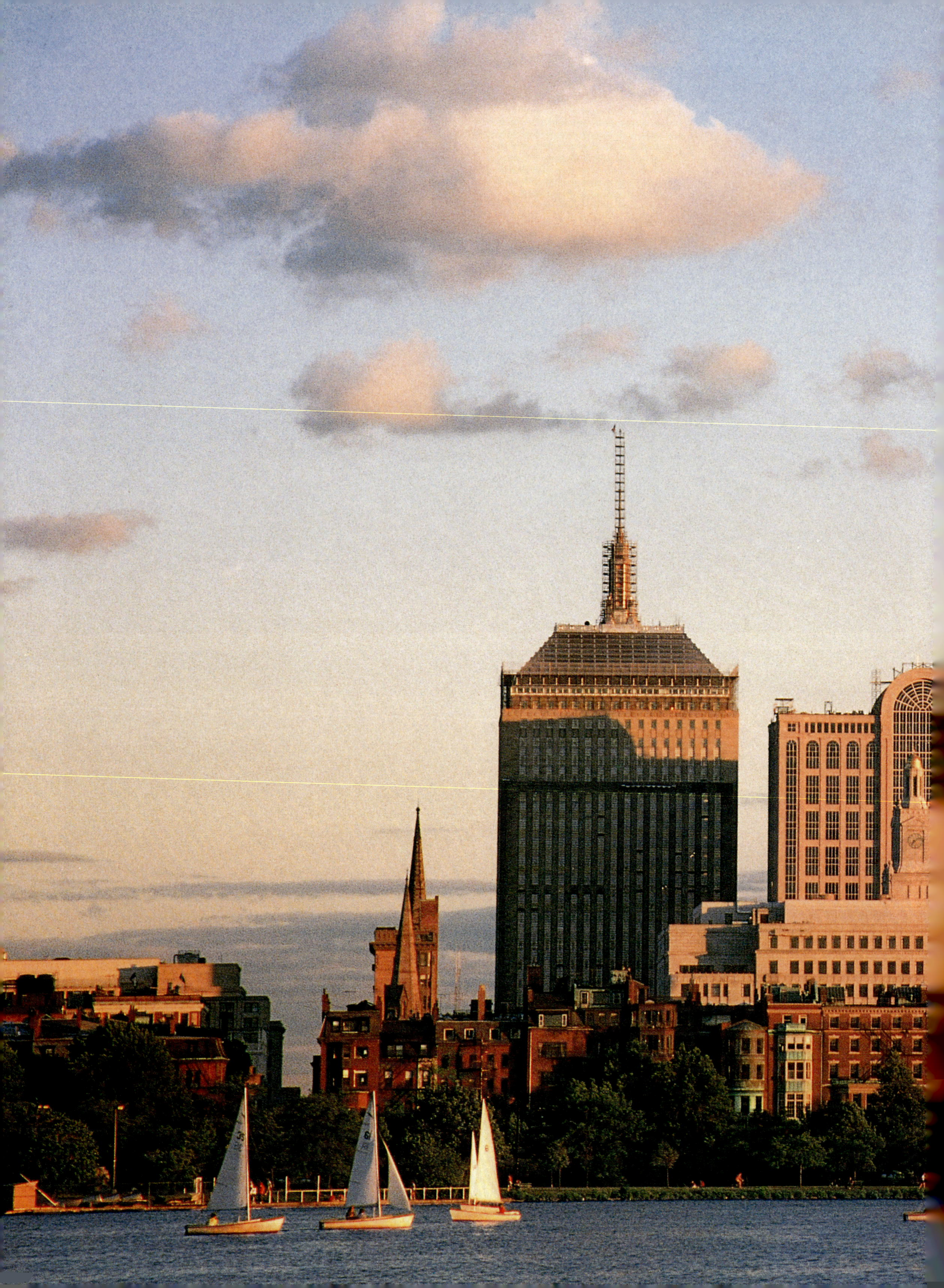

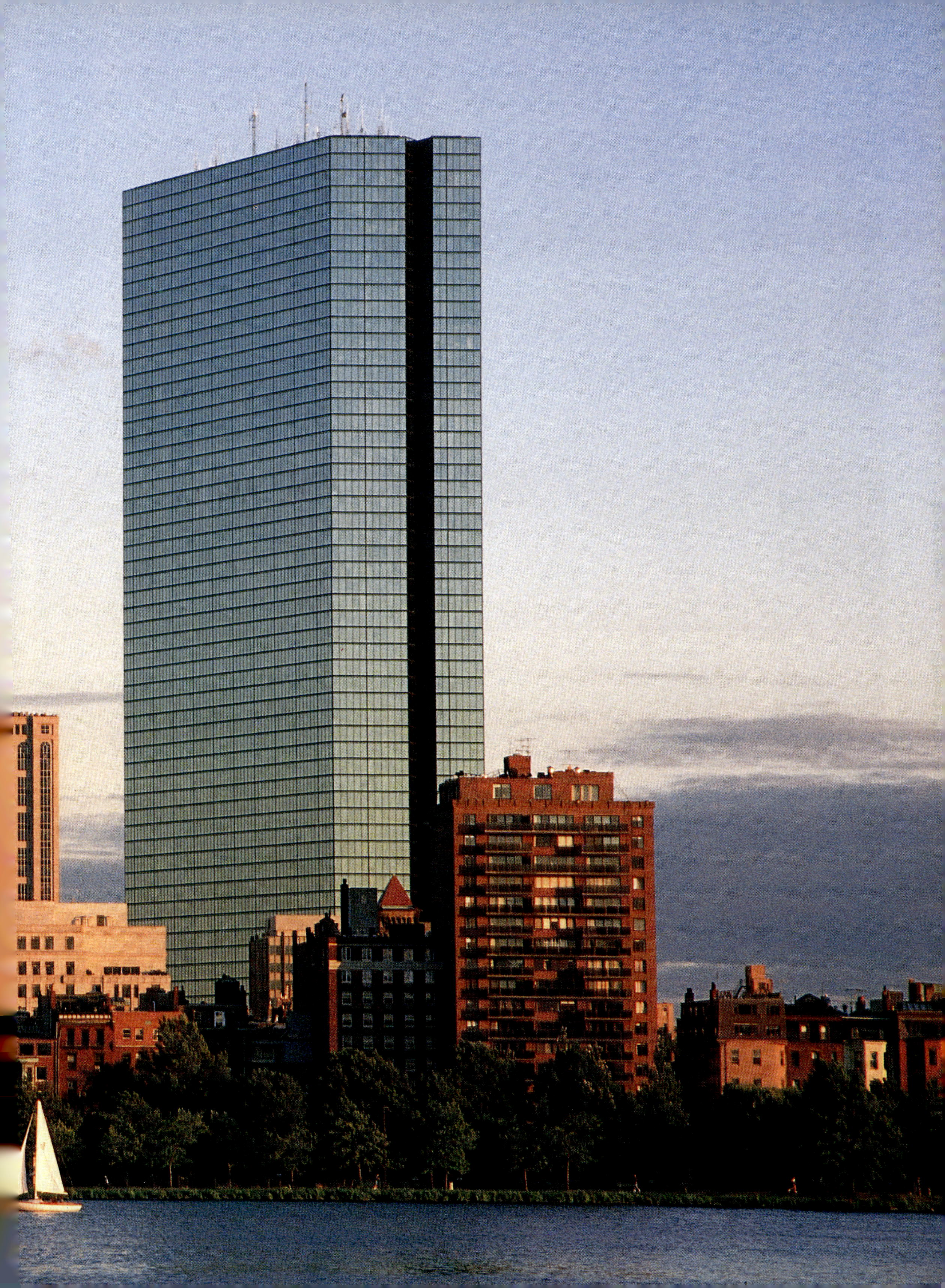

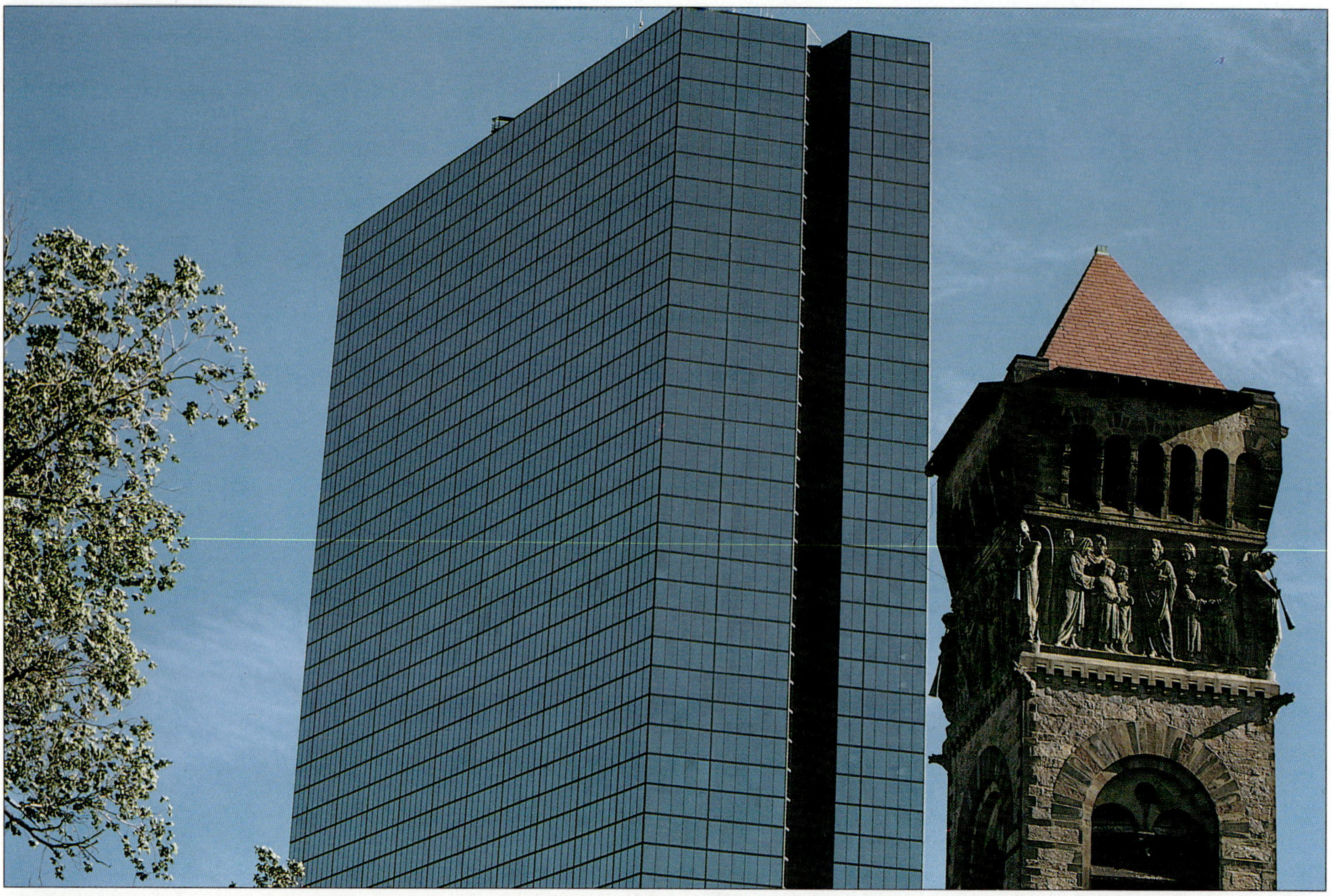

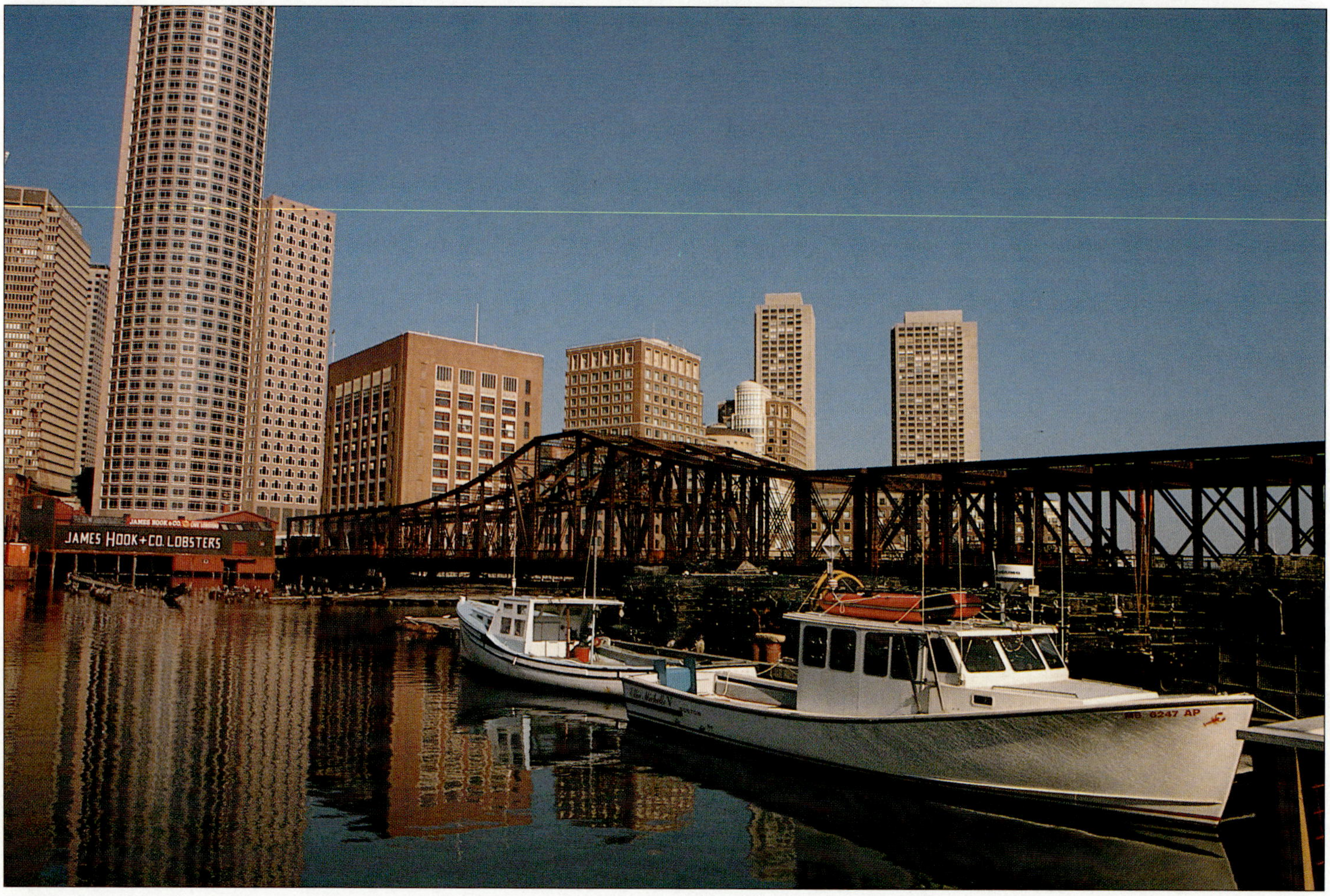
JAMES HOOK + CO. LOBSTERS

Facing page top: the spire of First Baptist Church beside Hancock Tower in Boston (these pages and overleaf). Facing page bottom: James Hook & Co. lobster boats on Boston's Waterfront. Above: the U.S.S. Constitution, *better known as "Old Ironsides." Above right: Harvard Yard, Harvard University, Cambridge. Right and overleaf: the Christian Science Center. Below right: New England Aquarium and Long Wharf. Below: Beaver II, replica of a "Tea Party" clipper.*

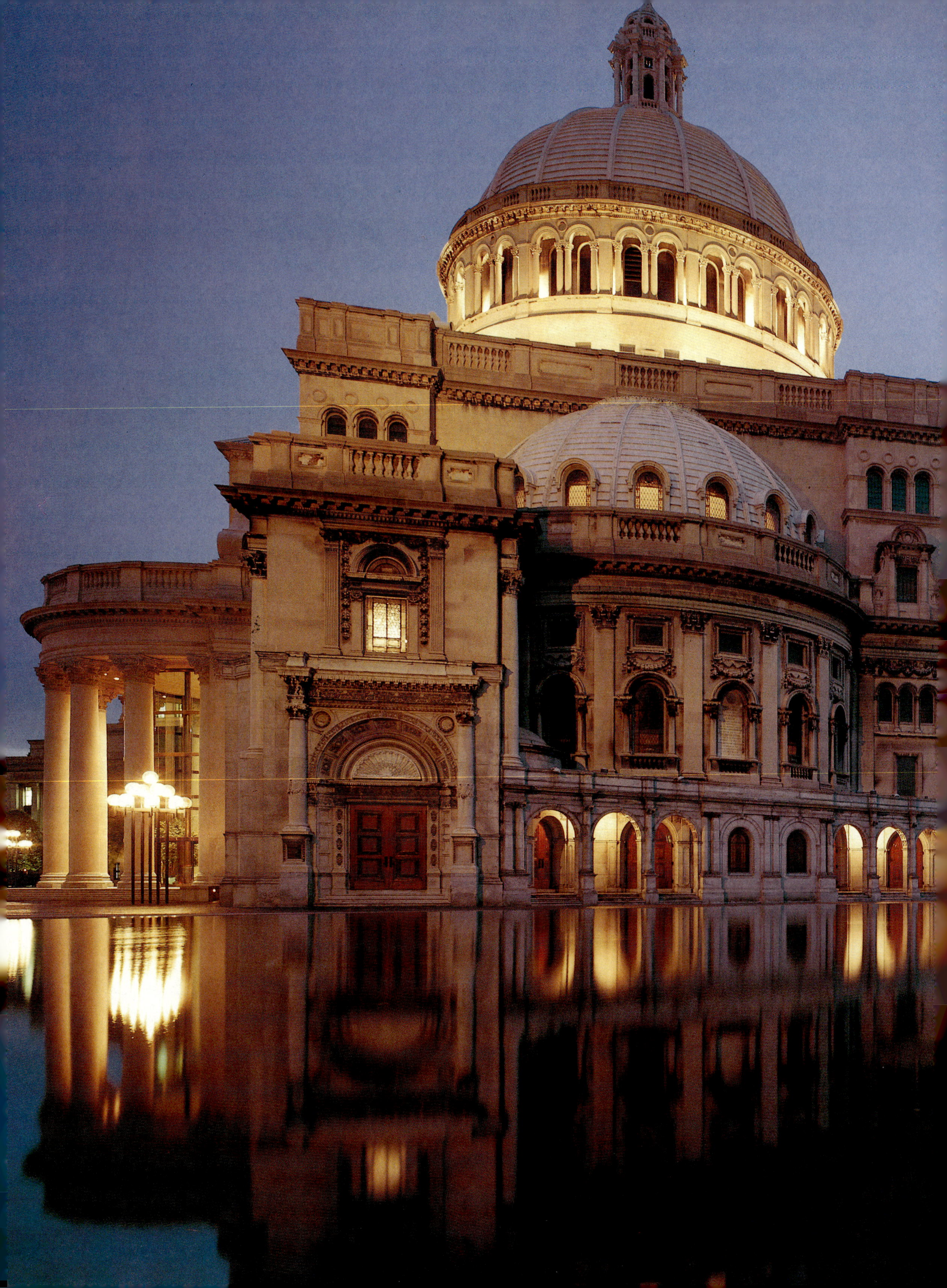

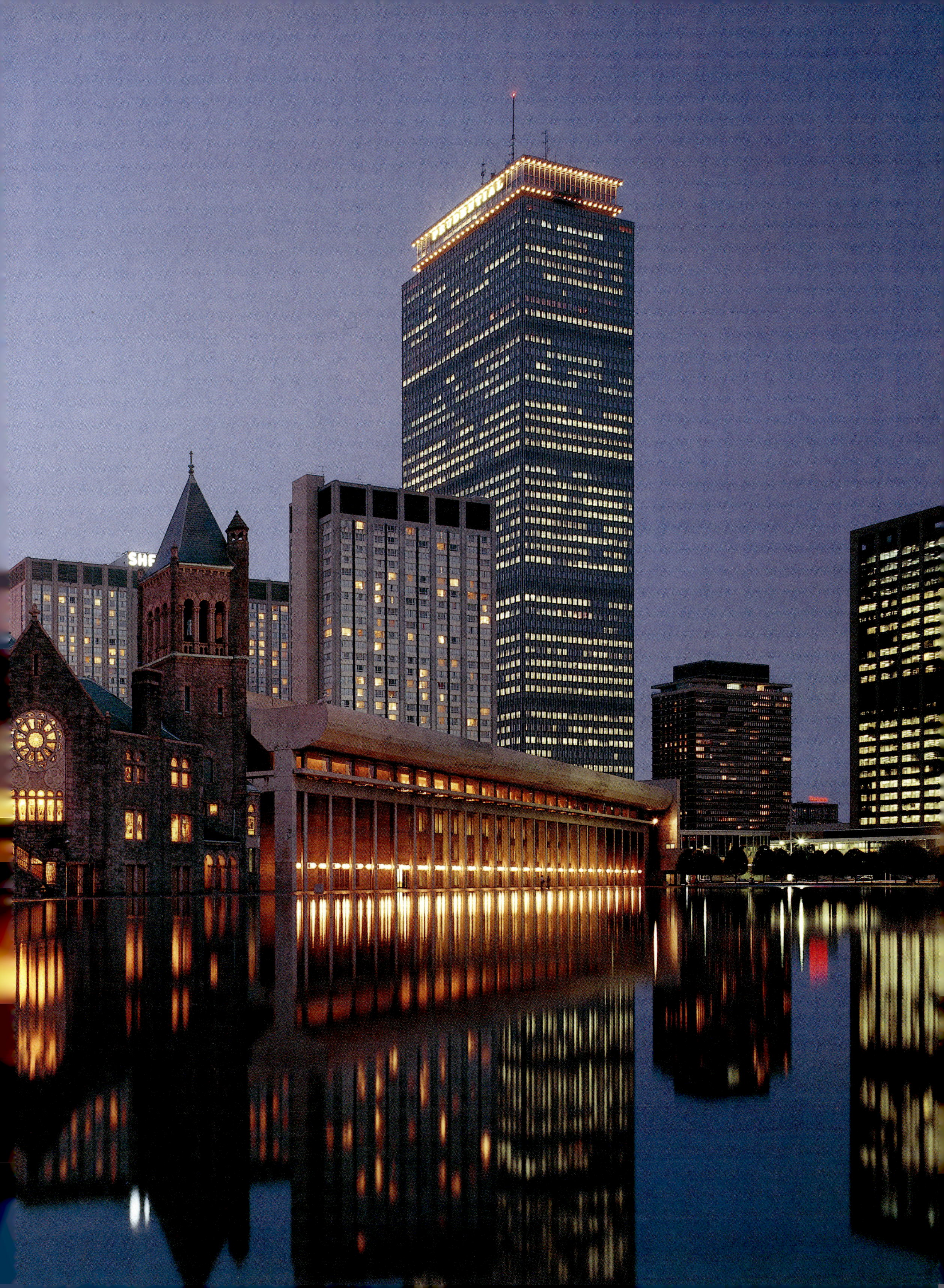

44

Facing page: (top) the Mayflower II, *moored at State Pier, and (bottom) the Plymouth Rock Memorial, both in Plymouth. The* Mayflower II *is a full-scale, 104-foot-long replica of the ship that brought the Pilgrims to America. Below: North Bridge, Concord. On the original "rude bridge that arched the flood," in Emerson's words, minutemen met British troops on April 19, 1775 and "fired the shot heard round the world."*

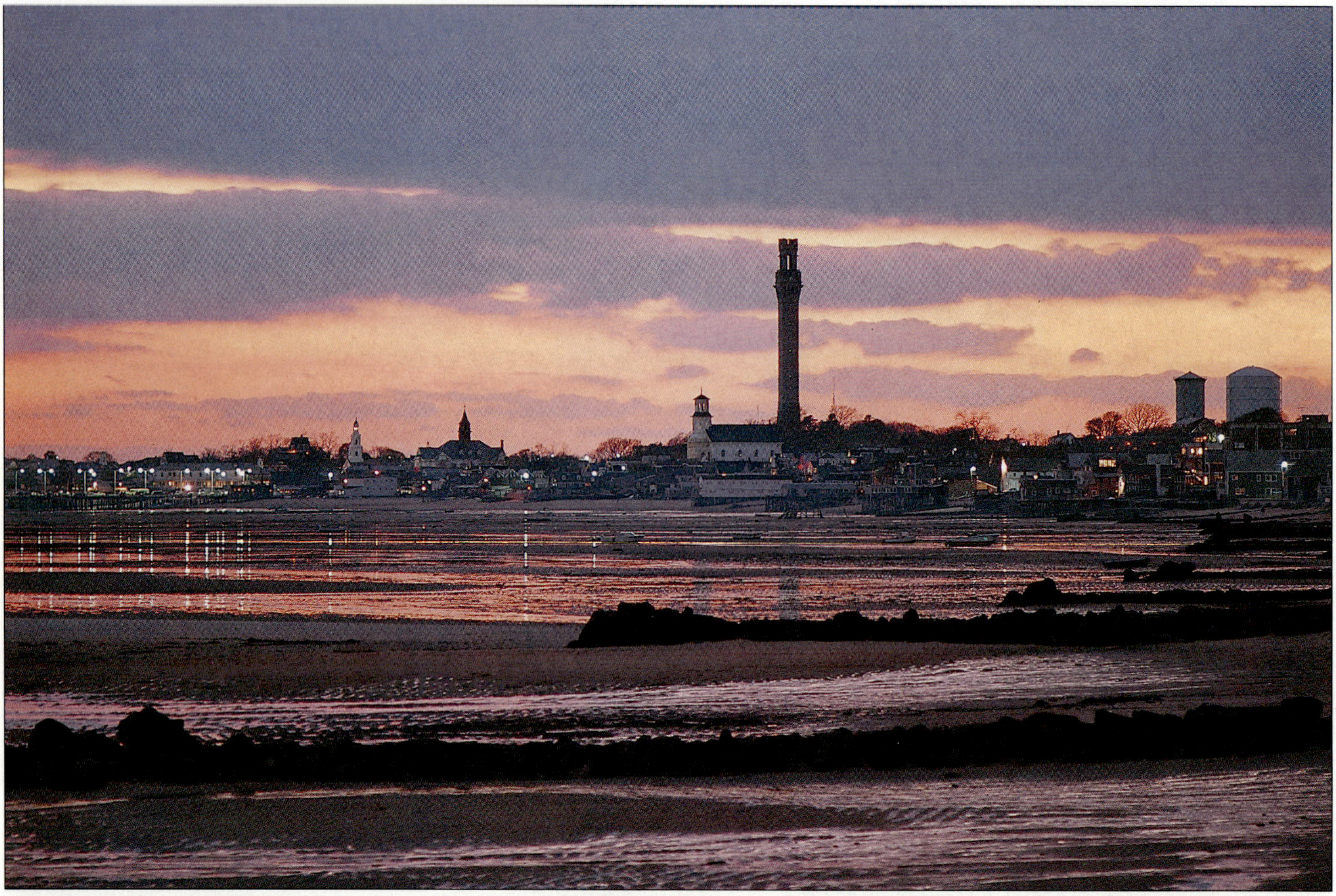

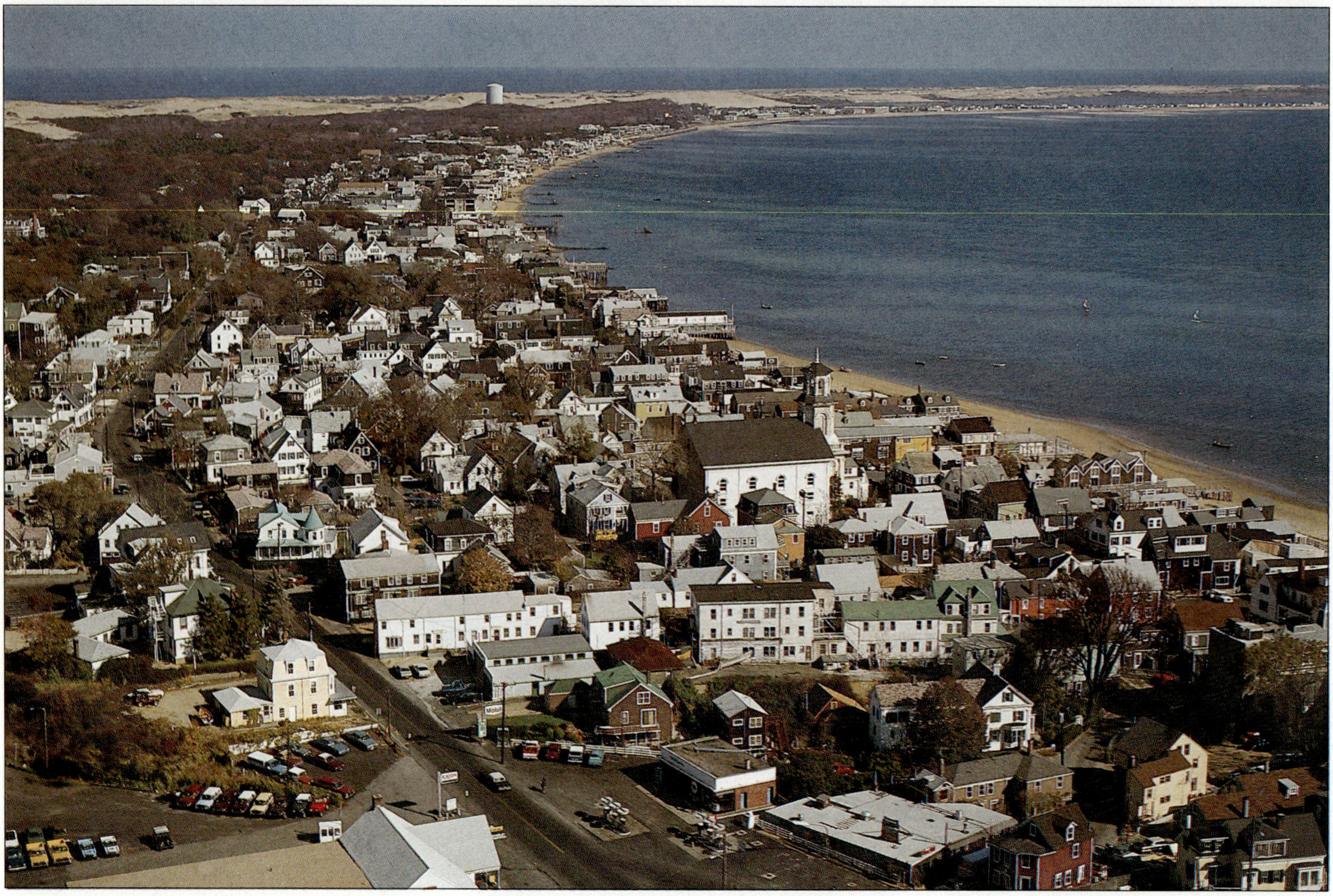

Facing page: (top) evening, mauve and violet, over Provincetown Harbor (bottom), Cape Cod (these pages and overleaf). The granite, 250-feet-high Pilgrim Monument stands tall against the sky in Provincetown. Above: the town hall in Brewster, and (above right) Martha's Vineyard. Right: Coast Guard Beach Center, Eastham. Below right: Nantucket Harbor. Below: Eastham Windmill, the oldest windmill on Cape Cod, built circa 1680. Overleaf: Mill Creek Marsh, Sandwich.

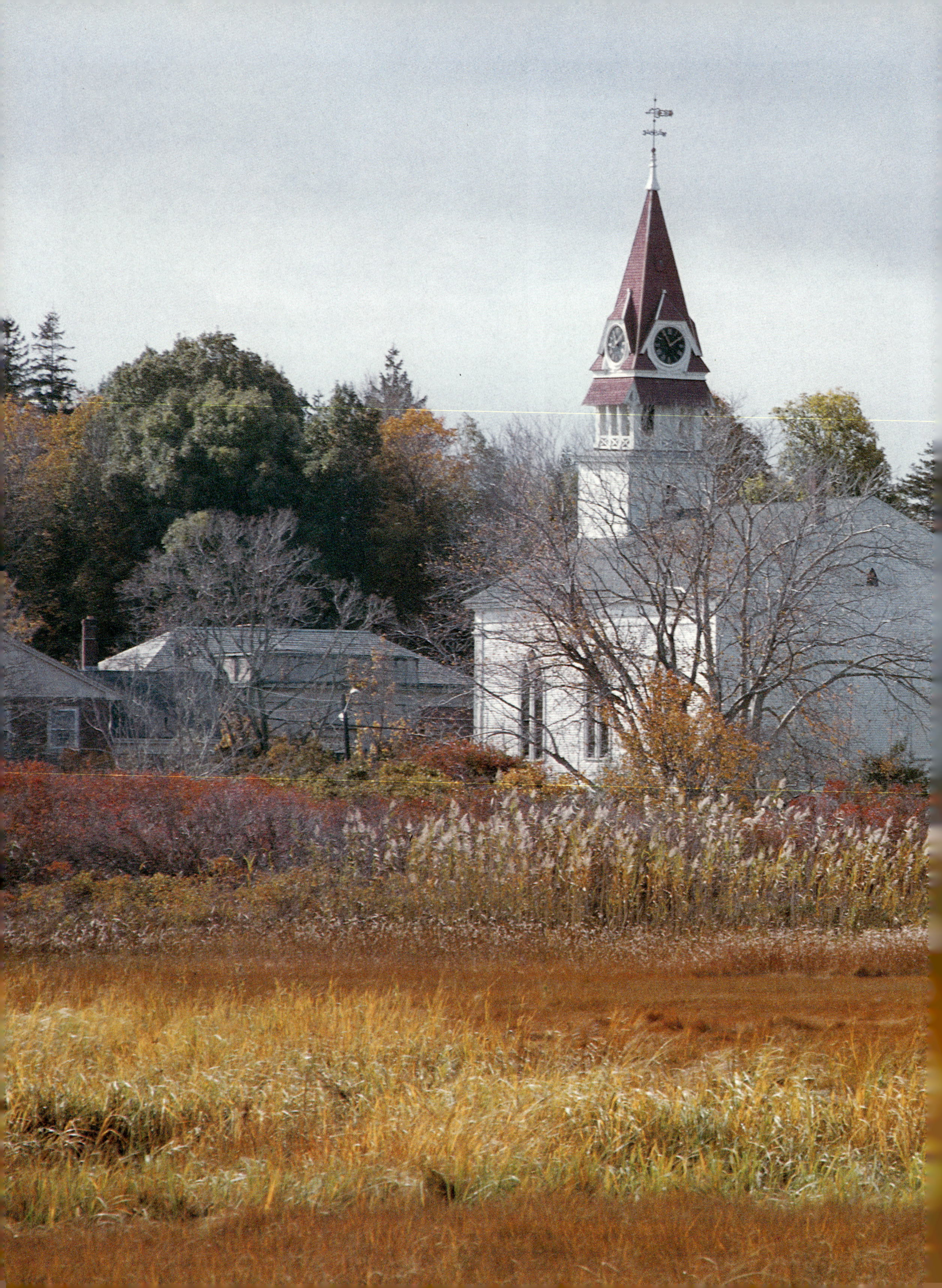

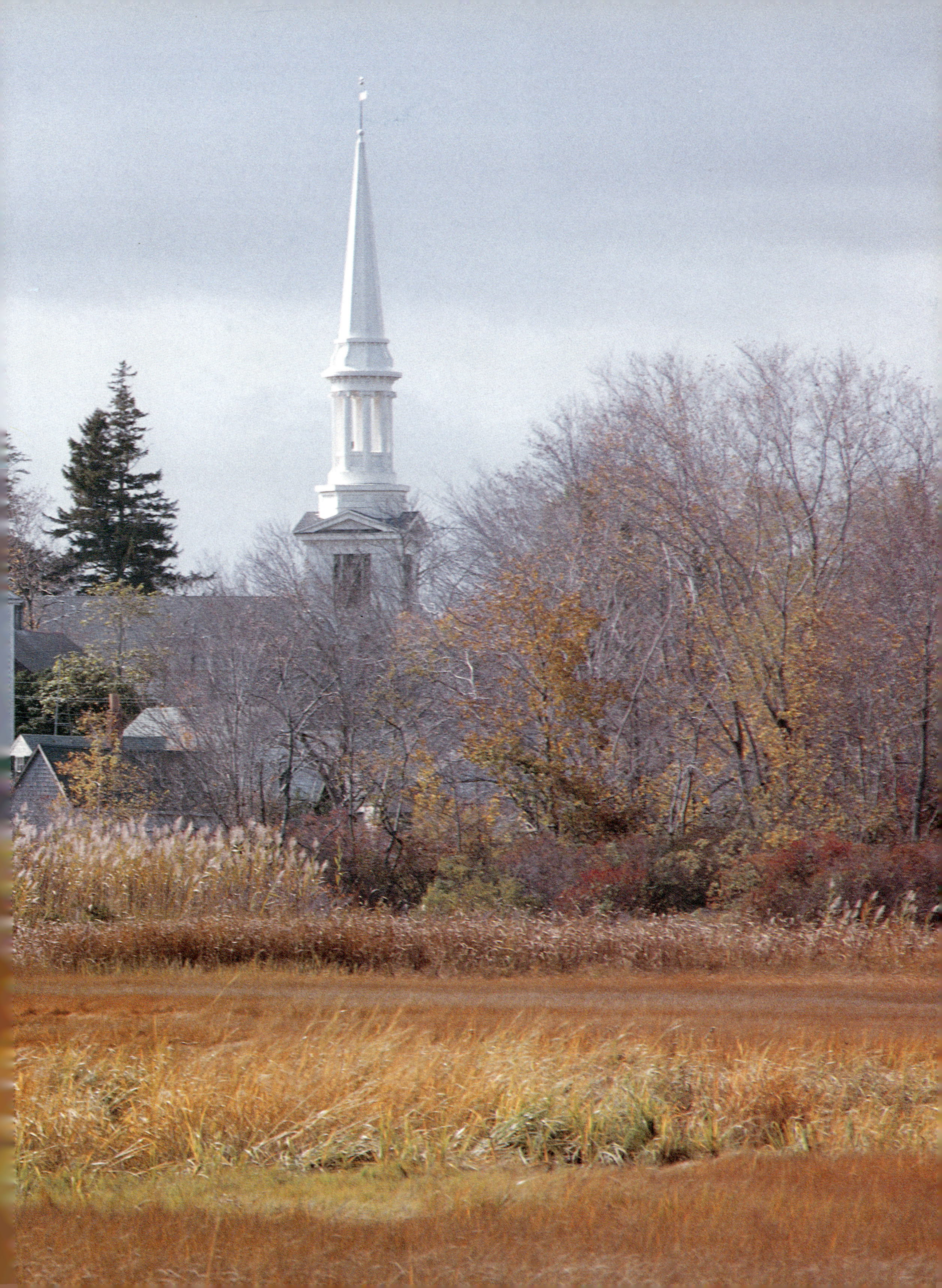

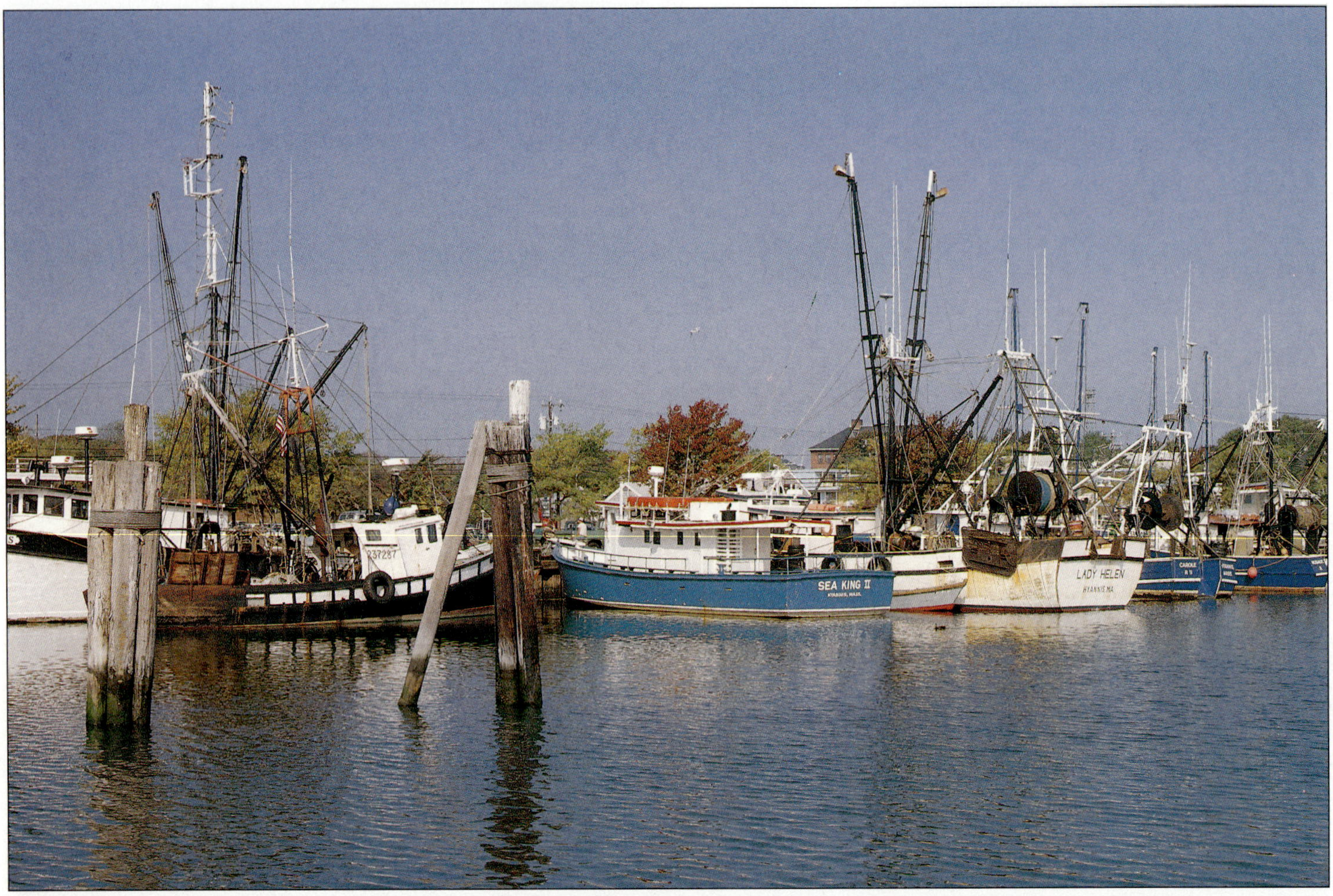
SEA KING II
LADY HELEN

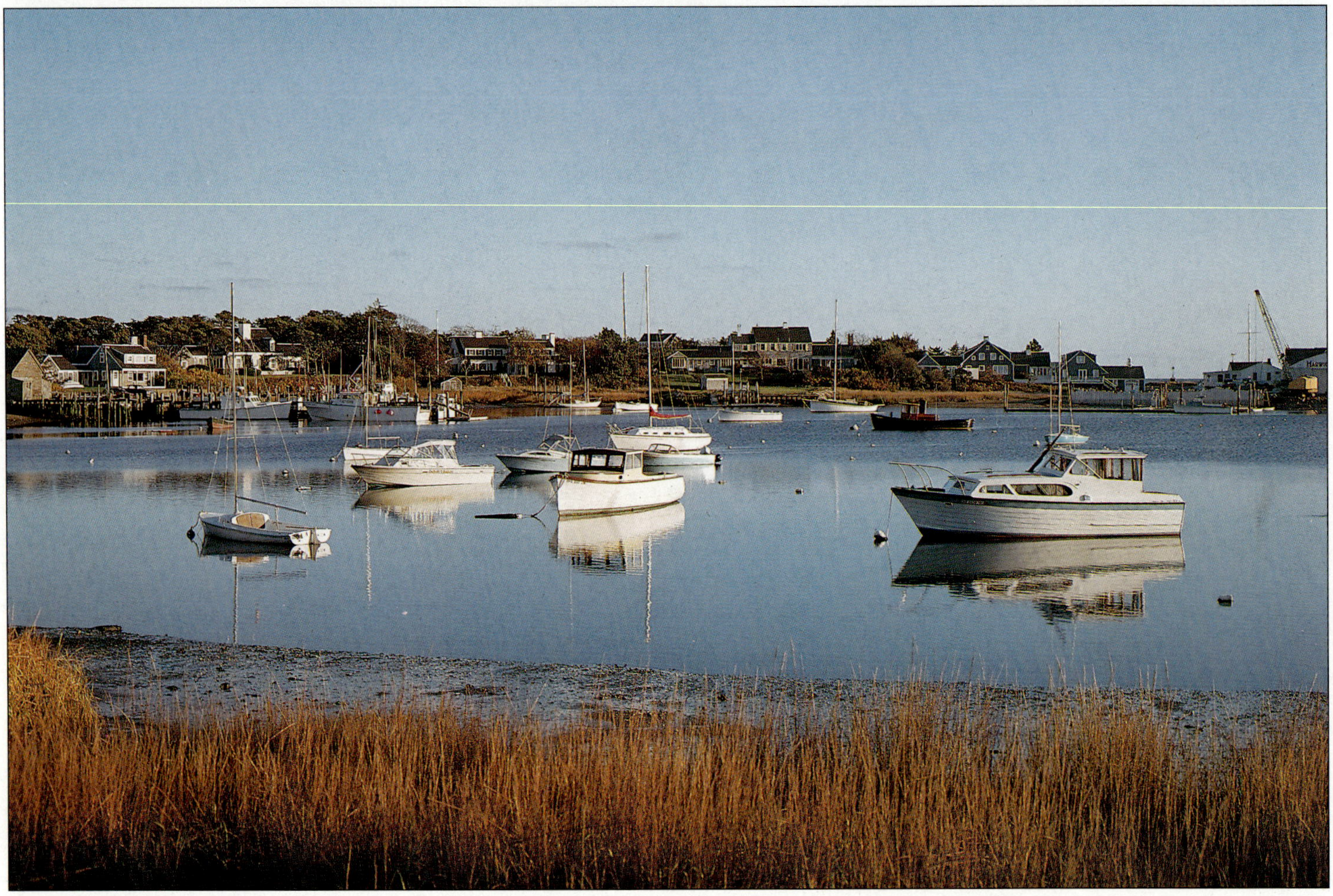

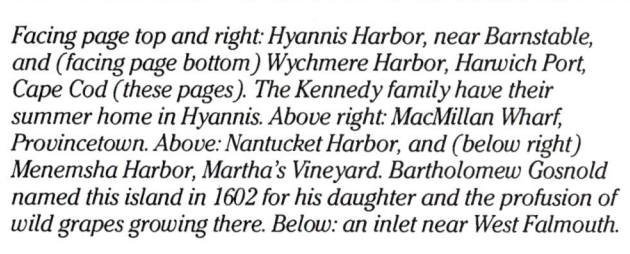

Facing page top and right: Hyannis Harbor, near Barnstable, and (facing page bottom) Wychmere Harbor, Harwich Port, Cape Cod (these pages). The Kennedy family have their summer home in Hyannis. Above right: MacMillan Wharf, Provincetown. Above: Nantucket Harbor, and (below right) Menemsha Harbor, Martha's Vineyard. Bartholomew Gosnold named this island in 1602 for his daughter and the profusion of wild grapes growing there. Below: an inlet near West Falmouth.

Above: dunes on Dionis Beach, Nantucket, Cape Cod. *Above left:* Nauset Light Beach, Cape Cod, and *(below left)* Province Lands near Provincetown, Cape Cod. *Facing page: (top)* Nauset Light, Cape Cod, and *(bottom)* Sankaty Head Lighthouse, Nantucket. *Overleaf:* Edgartown Light, Martha's Vineyard. Edgartown is the oldest settlement on Martha's Vineyard. *Left:* the cliffs of Gay Head, Martha's Vineyard, and *(below)* Nashaquitsa Cliffs, Gay Head, on Martha's Vineyard.

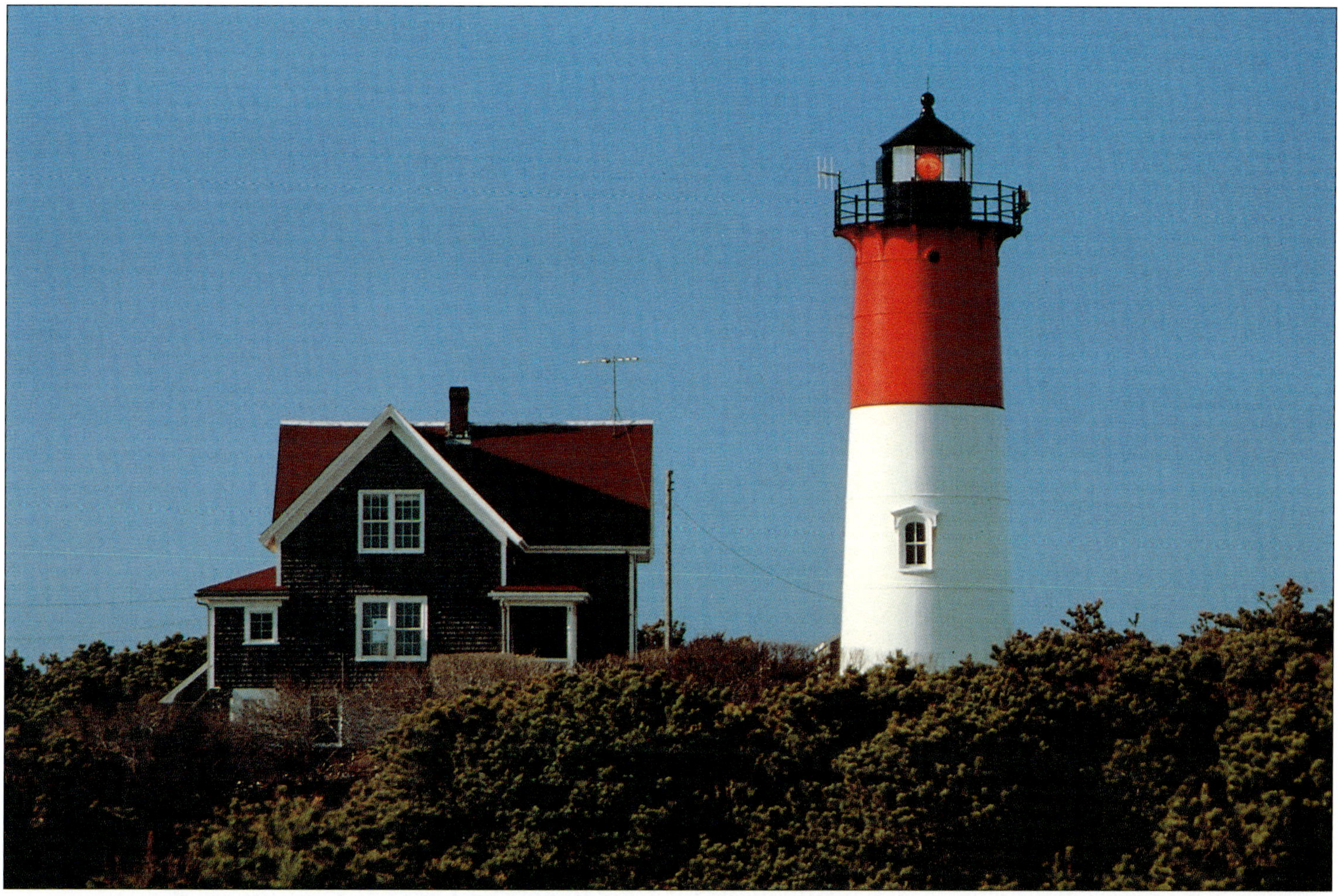

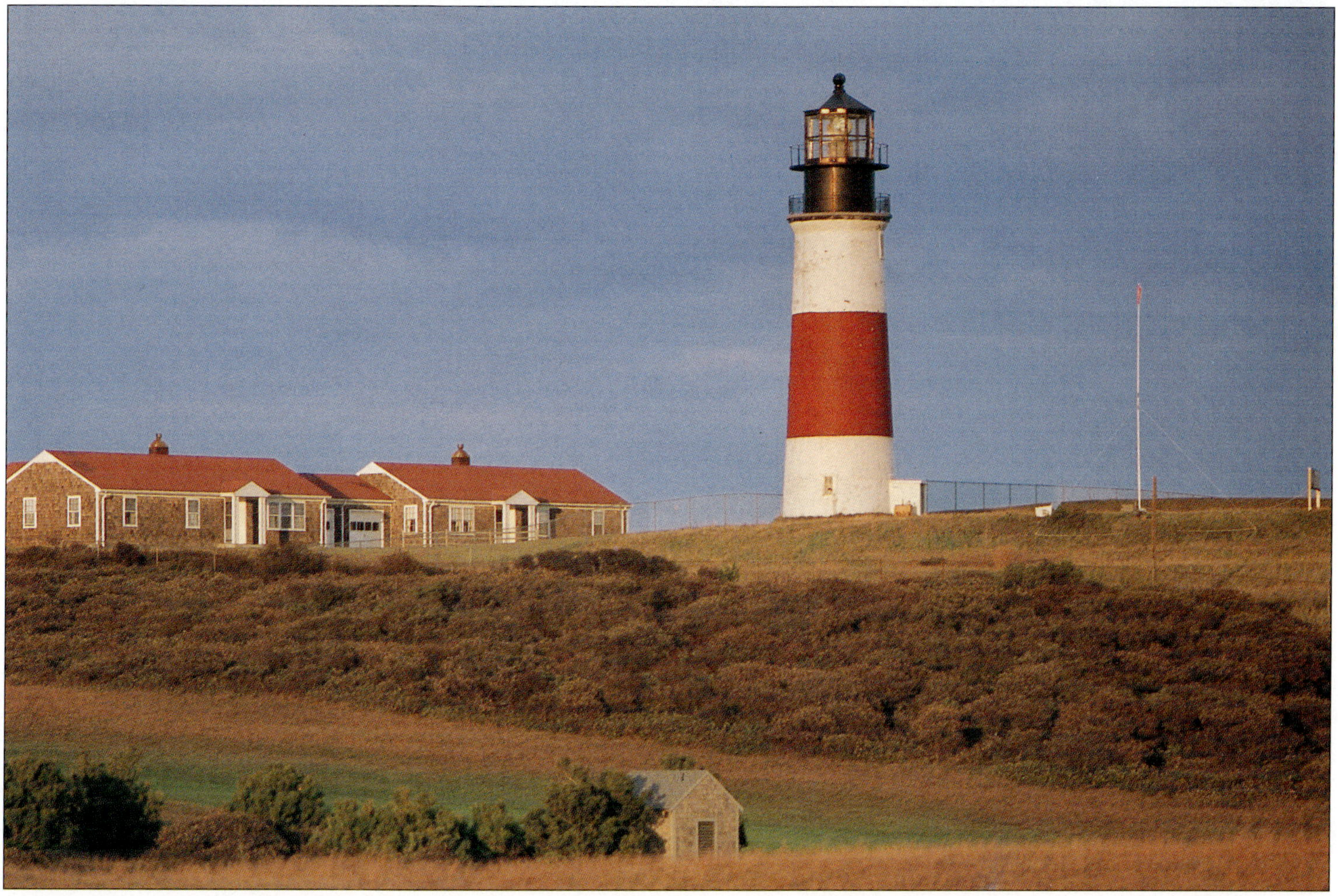

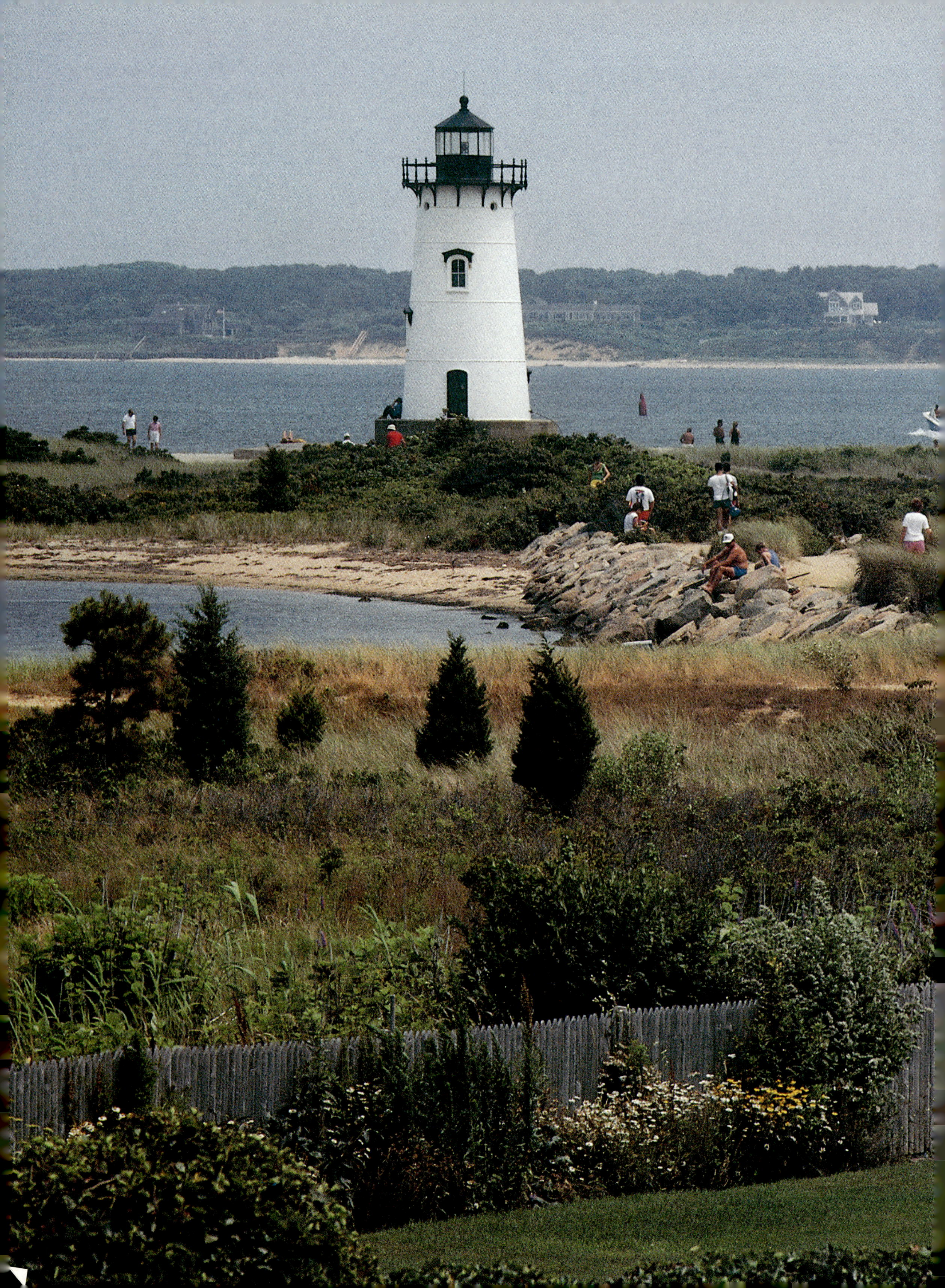

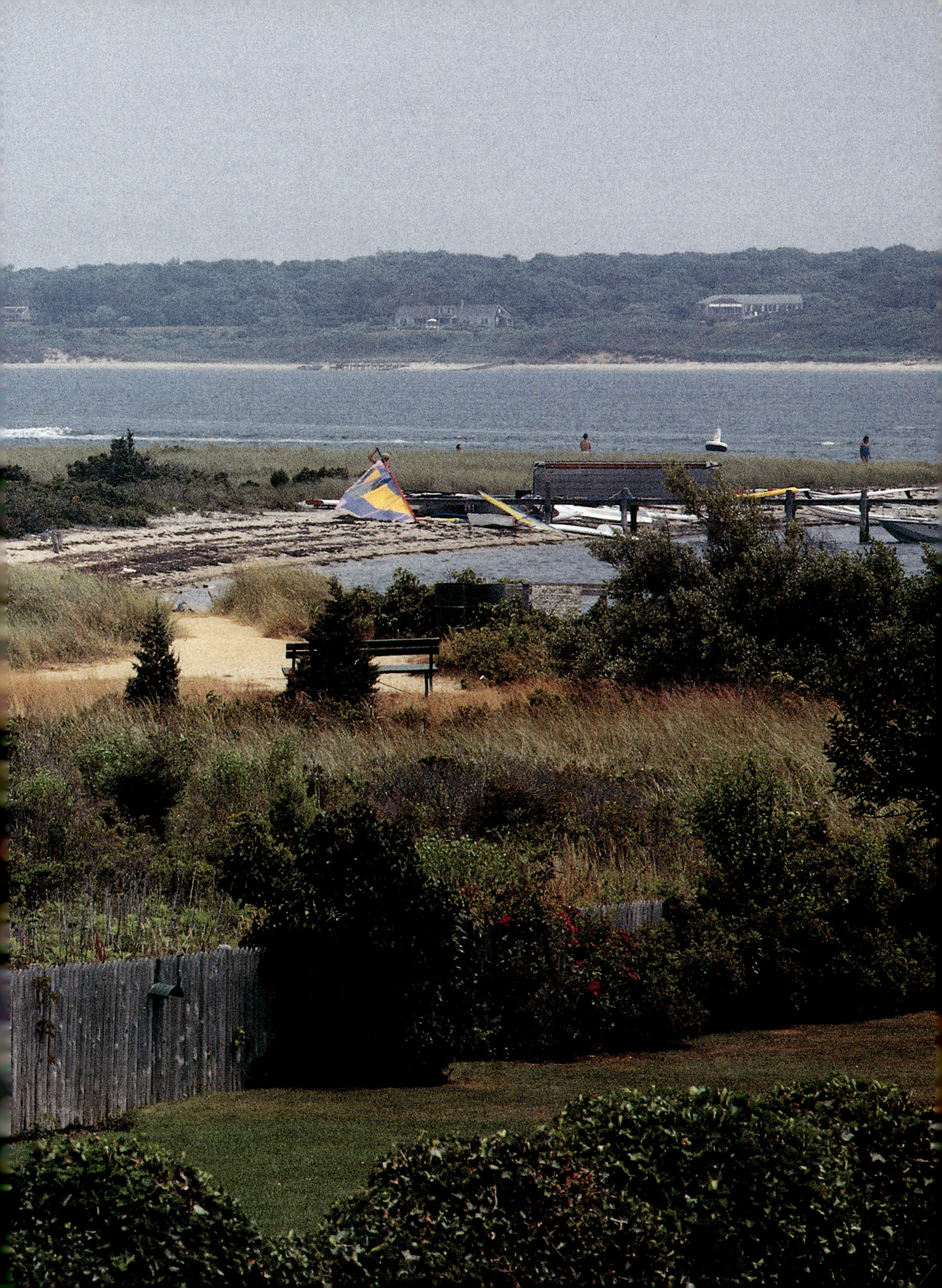

56

Facing page: (top) fishing at the Herring Run, Bourne, and (bottom) Hyannis Harbor. Above: a painter working in Edgartown, and (above right) South Beach, both in Martha's Vineyard. Right: the "On Time" Ferry, running from Edgartown to Chappaquiddick Island. Below right: Cape Cod Canal, Sandwich. Below: cranberry harvesting in a Nantucket cranberry bog. Overleaf: the Atlantic seen from Nauset Light Beach, part of the National Seashore, Eastham.

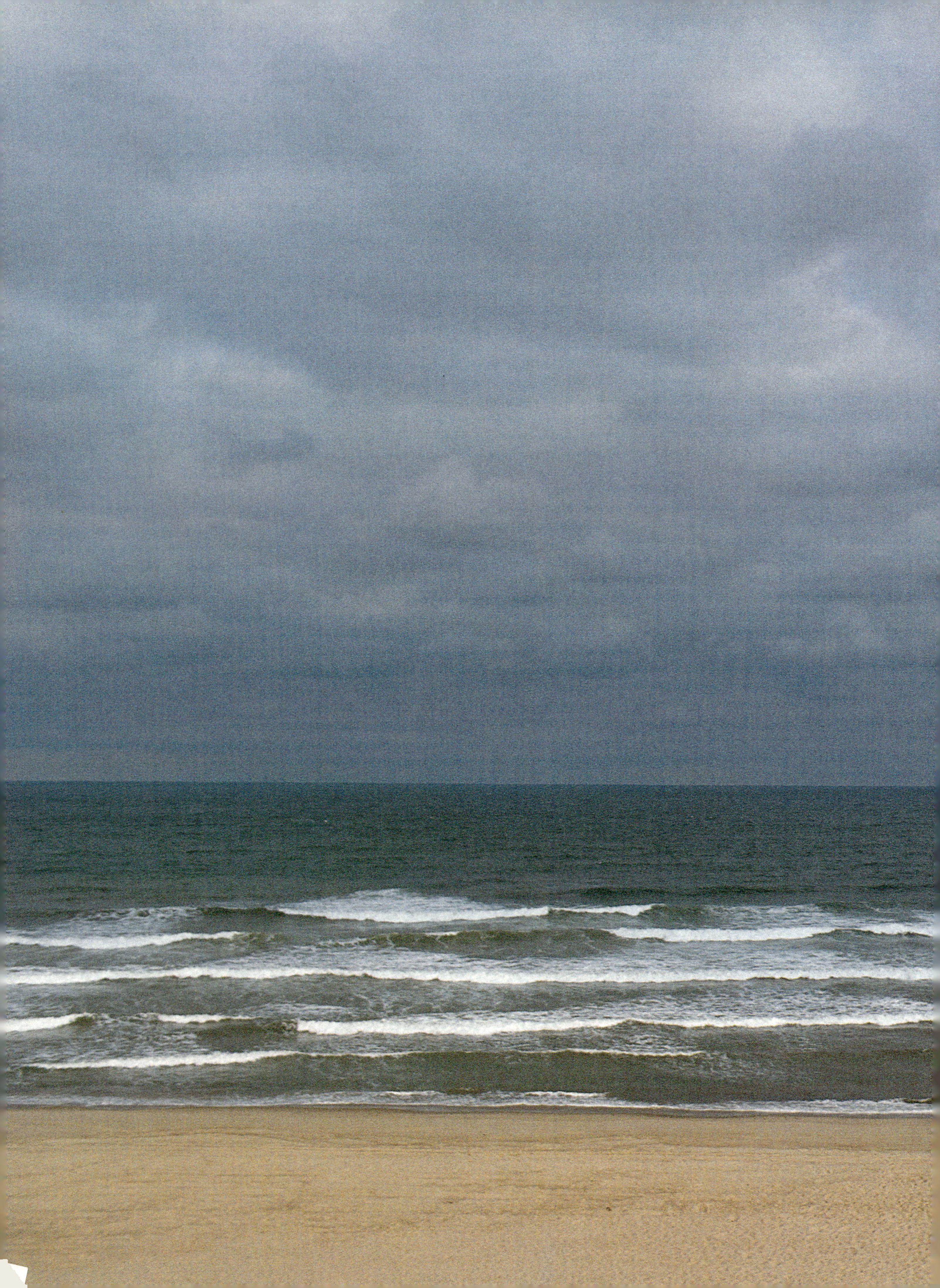

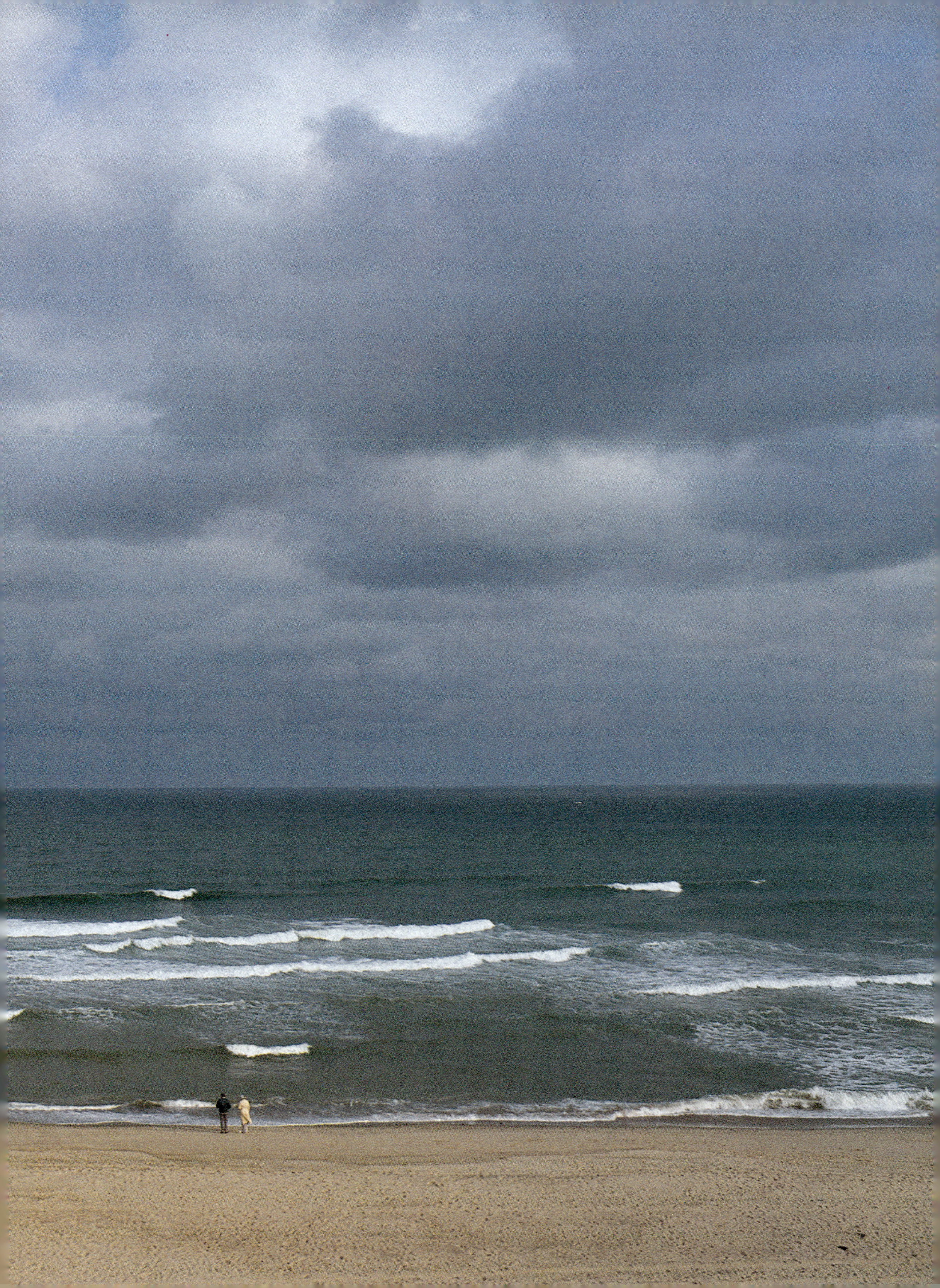

These pages: the beautiful beaches of Massachusetts. Overleaf: Herring Cove, and (following page) Westport.

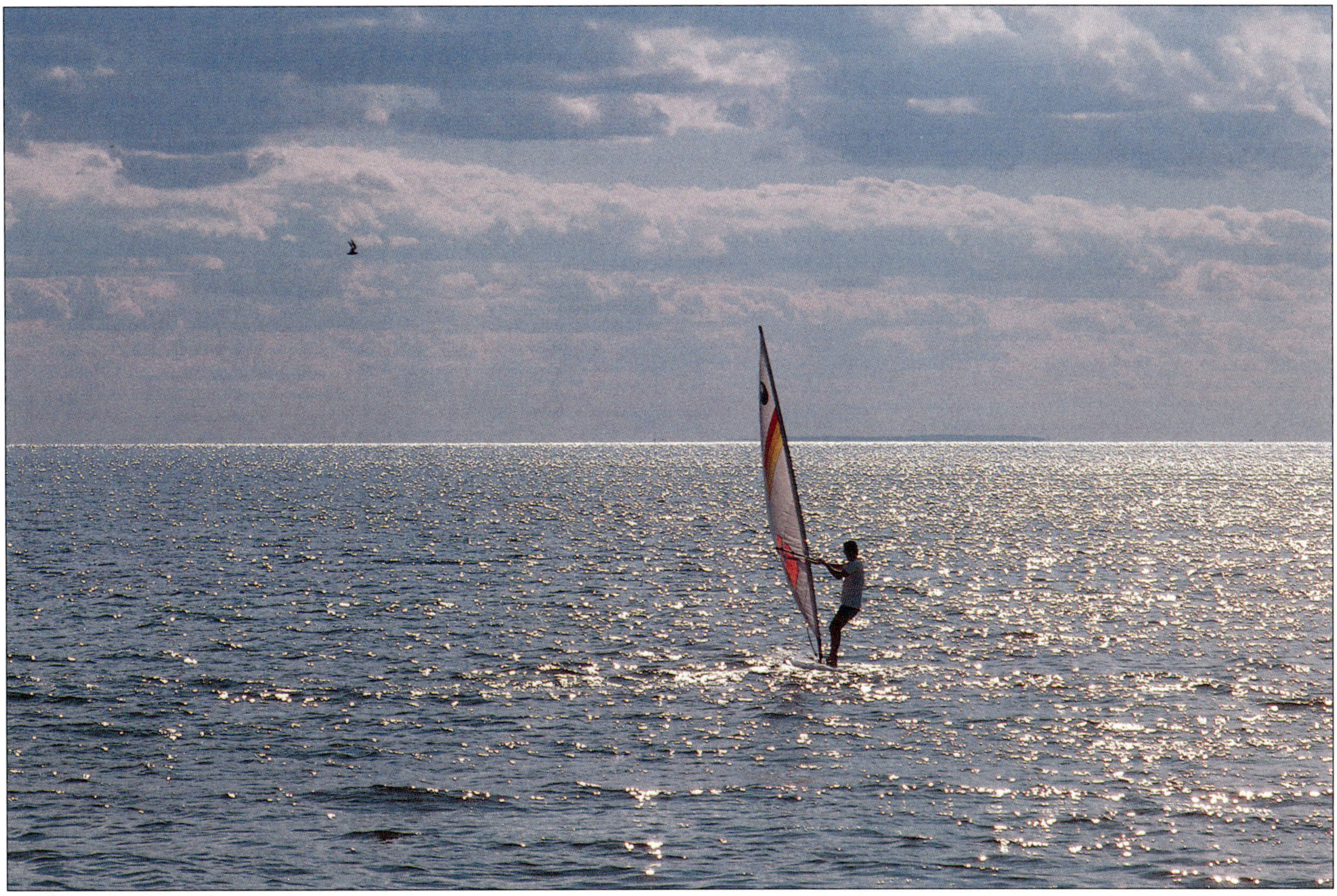

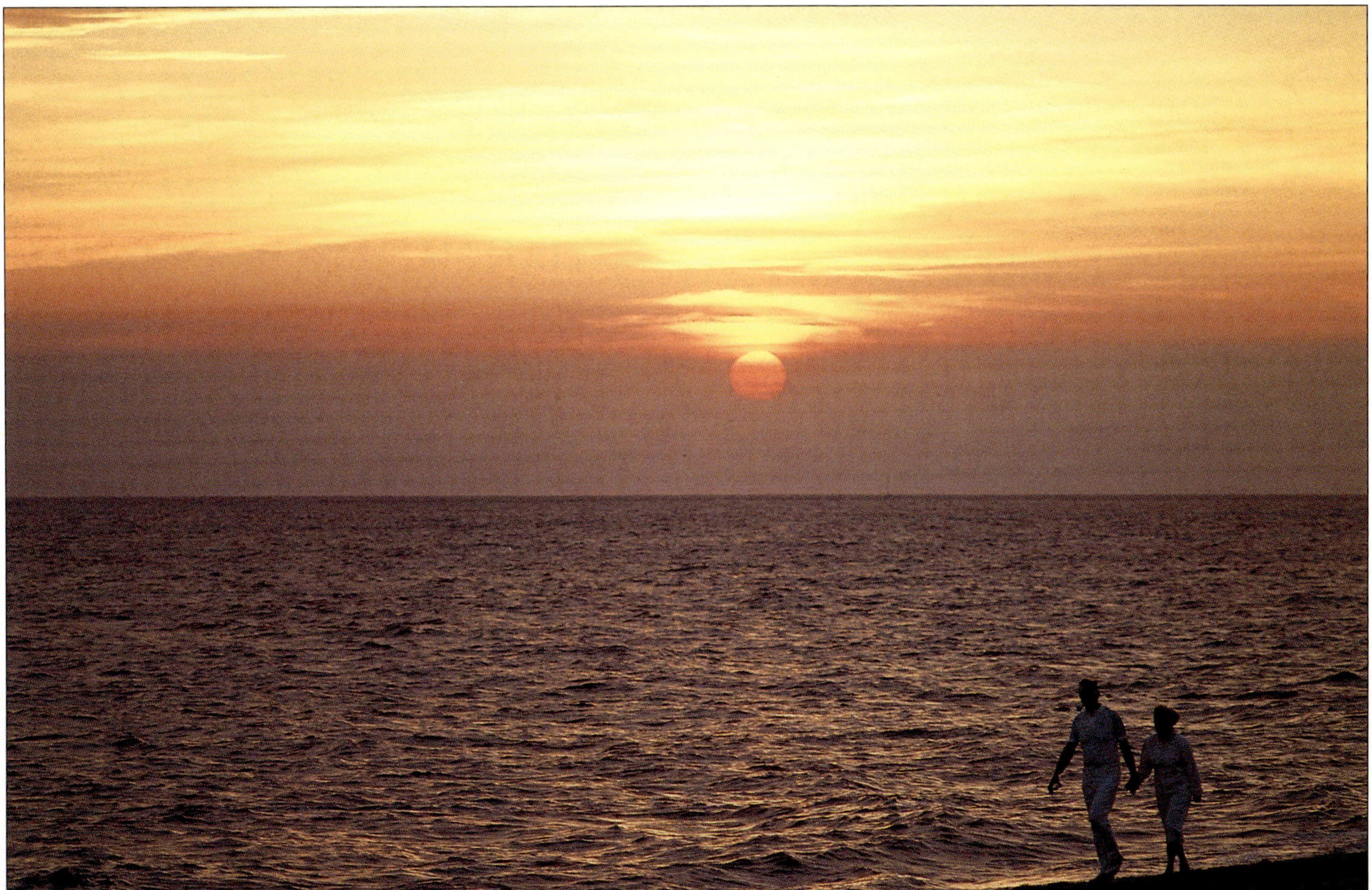

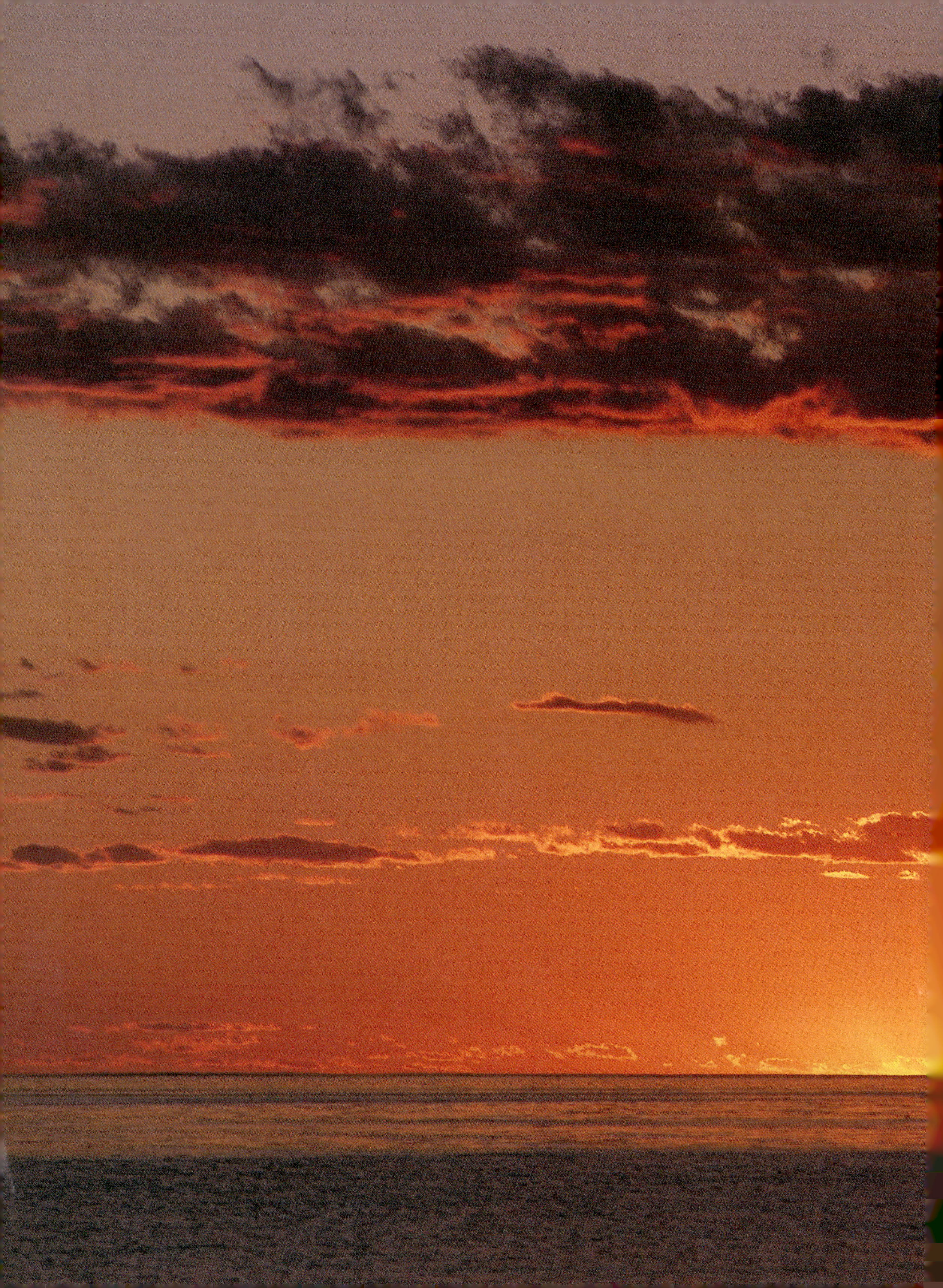